D1452067

Kol Dodi Dofek
Listen – My Beloved Knocks

Rabbi Joseph B. Soloveitchik

Kol Dodi Dofek
Listen – My Beloved Knocks

translated and annotated
by
David Z. Gordon

edited
by
Jeffrey R. Woolf

A Publication of Yeshiva University

Library of Congress Cataloging-in-Publication Data

Soloveitchik, Joseph Dov.
  [Ḳol dodi dofeḳ. English]
  Listen my beloved knocks / Joseph B. Soloveitchik ; translated and annotated by
David Z. Gordon ; edited by Jeffrey R. Woolf.
  p. cm.
  Includes bibliographical references.
  ISBN 0-88125-897-0
  1. Israel and the diaspora. 2. Jews--United States--Attitudes toward Israel.
  3. Suffering--Religious aspects--Judaism. 4. Covenants--Religious aspects--Judaism.
  5. Jews--Identity. 6. Zionism. I. Gordon, David Z. II. Woolf, Jeffrey R. III. Title.
DS132.S6513 2005
296.3'1173--dc22
                                                                    2005027762

This essay originated as an address delivered in Yiddish by the author to the Religious Zionists of America on the occasion of the Eighth Anniversary (May, 1956) of Israel's independence. It was subsequently elaborated upon, rewritten in Hebrew and appeared in an anthology entitled "*Torah U-Meluchah*" published in Jerusalem in 1961.

This translation was completed in March of 1990.

Table of Contents

KOL DODI DOFEK
LISTEN – MY BELOVED KNOCKS [A]

[A] Song of Songs 5:2. The translation is per Ibn Ezra, Genesis 4:10 s.v. *Tzoakim Eilai.*

This work contains 23 footnotes by the author. As some of them are lengthy, they all appear at the end of the translation. These footnotes are indicated in the text by Arabic numerals. The translator's annotations appear at the bottom of each page and are denoted by capital letters beginning with A *et seq* in each section. References in the text to verses in the Bible, quotations from the Talmud and all other Jewish sources have been inserted by the translator and appear in parenthesis in the text.

—Trans.

Chapter 1
The Righteous Suffer

One of the deepest of mysteries, troubling Judaism from the dawn of its existence, is the problem of suffering. At a propitious moment of Divine compassion, Moses, the master of all prophets, pleaded before the Lord of All to be enlightened as to the workings of this impenetrable phenomenon.[1] Moses knocked on the gates of heaven and cried out, "Show me now Your ways, that I shall comprehend You, so that I might find grace in Your eyes . . . instruct me as to Your glory" (Exodus 33:13, 18).

Why and wherefore are hardships visited on man? Why and wherefore do the righteous suffer and evildoers prosper? From that wondrous morning when Moses, the faithful shepherd, communed with the Creator of the Universe and pleaded for the comprehensive solution to this question of questions, throughout the generations, the prophets and sages of Israel have grappled with this conundrum. Habakkuk demanded satisfaction for this affront to justice; Jeremiah, King David in his Psalms, and Solomon in Ecclesiastes all pondered this problem. The Book of Job is totally dedicated to this ancient riddle that still hovers over our world and demands its own resolu-

1

tion:Why does the Holy One, blessed be He,[A] permit evil
to have dominion over His creations?

Judaism, in quest for a safe harbor in a world split and
dismembered by existential suffering, and in its search
for a solution to the mystery of the suffering that (to all
outward appearances) pervades without limits, came to
a new formulation and definition of this problem that
has both greater breadth and greater depth. Posing the
question of suffering, claims Judaism, is possible in two
separate dimensions: the dimension of fate and the
dimension of destiny. Judaism has always distinguished
between an "Existence of Fate" and an "Existence of
Destiny," between the "I" which is the progeny of fate
and the "I" which is the child of destiny. In this distinc-
tion lies hidden the Jewish doctrine of suffering.

What is an Existence of Fate? It is an existence of
duress, in the nature of "against your will do you live" (M.
Avot 4:29).[2] It is a factual existence, simply one line in a
[long] chain of mechanical causality, devoid of significance, direction, and purpose, and subordinate to the
forces of the environment into whose midst the individual is pushed, unconsulted by Providence. The "I" of fate
emerges as an object. As an object, man appears as acted
upon and not as actor. He is acted upon through his passive collision with the objective outside, as one object
confronting another. The "I" of fate is hurled into a sealed
dynamic that is always turned outward. Man's existence

[A] Hereinafter "the Holy One."

is hollow, lacking inner content, substance, and independence. The "I" of fate denies itself completely, because the sense of selfhood and objectification cannot dwell in tandem.

It is against such a background that the experience of evil surfaces in all its terror. There are two stages in fate/existence. From the start, the man/object, imprisoned, against his will, [bound up] in the chains of existence, stands perplexed and confused in the face of the great mystery called suffering. Fate mocks him: his existence, crazed and torn, opposes itself and denies its worth and importance. The fear of extinction assails him and crushes his body and soul. The sufferer wanders lost in the vacuousness of the world, with God's fear spread over him and his anger tensed against it; he is entirely shaken and agitated. His agonies are devoid of any clear meaning and they appear as satanic forces, as outgrowths of the primal chaos that pollutes the creation whose destiny it was to be a reflection of the Creator. At this stage of perplexity and speechlessness, of numbness of the heart and confusion of the mind, man does not ask at all about the reason for evil and its essence. He simply suffers in silence and is choked by his anguish, which silences his complaint and suppresses questioning and inquiry.

After the psychic quaking of the sufferer, which comes as a first reaction to suffering, comes the intellectual curiosity of the sufferer, which seeks to understand existence and to strengthen the sufferer's safety and security. At this stage man begins to examine suffering and to ask weighty questions. He searches for the rational foundations of suffering and evil, and he endeavors to find the tranquility and harmony that lie between the positive and negative and thus to remove the edge from the tension between the thesis, "good," and the antithesis, "evil," of existence. From the question and the inquiry, the solution and the answer, he arrives at a metaphysical formulation of evil through which he comes to terms with evil and attempts to gloss it over. The sufferer employs the powers of rational abstraction (with which the Creator endowed him) to the point of self-deception: denial of the existence of evil in the world.

Judaism, with its realistic approach to man and his status within existence, understood that evil does not lend itself to being obscured and glossed over, and that every attempt to diminish the import of the contrast and cleavage in existence will not bring man to inner peace or to comprehension of the existential secret. Evil is a fact that cannot be denied. There is evil in the world. There are suffering and agony, and death pangs. He who would deceive himself by ignoring the split in existence and by romanticizing life is but a fool and a fabricator of illusions. It is impossible to conquer monstrous evil with philosophical-speculative thought. Thus, Judaism determined that man, submerged in the depths of a frozen fate, will in vain seek the solution to the problem of evil in the context of speculative thought, for he will never find it. Certainly, the testimony of the Torah regarding creation — that "it is very good" (Genesis 1:12) — is true. However, this is only stated from the unbounded perspective of the Creator. In man's finite, limited view, the absolute good in creation is not apparent. The contrast is striking and undeniable. There is evil that is not susceptible to explanation and comprehension. Only by comprehending the world in its totality can man gain insight into the essence of suffering. However, as long as man's perception is limited and fragmented, so that he sees only isolated portions of the cosmic drama and the mighty saga of history, he cannot delve into the recesses of evil and the mystery of suffering. To what might this situation be compared? To a person who views a beautiful tapestry, the work of a fine artisan, which contains, woven into it on its front, a representation dazzling to the eye. To our great sorrow, we see this image [i.e., the world] from the obverse side. Can such a sight become a sublime esthetic experience? Thus, we are incapable of comprehending the panorama of reality without which one cannot uncover God's master plan — the essence of the works of the Holy One.

In short, the "I" of fate asks a speculative/ metaphysical question about evil, and this question is not given to solution and has no answer.

In the second dimension of man's existence, destiny, the question of suffering takes on new form. What is an Existence of Destiny? It is an active existence, when man confronts the environment into which he has been cast with an understanding of his uniqueness and value, freedom and capacity; without compromising his integrity and independence in his struggle with the outside world. The slogan of the "I" of destiny is: "Against your will you are born, and against your will you die" (M. Avot 4:29), but by your free will do you live. Man is born as an object, dies as an object, but it is within his capability to live as a "subject" — as a creator and innovator who impresses his individual imprimatur on his life and breaks out of a life of instinctive, automatic behavior into one of creative activity. According to Judaism, man's mission in this world is to turn fate into destiny — an existence that is passive and influenced into an existence that is active and influential; an existence of compulsion, perplexity, and speechlessness into an existence full of will, vision, and initiative. The blessing of the Holy One to his creation fully defines man's role: "Be fruitful and multiply and replenish the earth and subdue it" (Genesis 1:28). Conquer the environment and subjugate it. If you do not rule over it, it will enslave you. Destiny bestows on man a new status in God's world. It bestows upon man a royal crown, and thus he becomes God's partner in the work of creation.

As stated above, in man's "Existence of Destiny" arises a new relation to the problem of evil. As long as man vacillates in his fateful existence, his relationship to evil is expressed solely in a philosophical/speculative approach. As a passive creature, it was not within his power to wrestle with evil in order to contain or to exploit it for an exalted purpose. The child of fate is devoid of the ability to determine anything in the realm of his existence. He is nurtured from the outside, and his life bears its imprint. Therefore he relates to evil from an impractical perspective and philosophizes about it from a speculative point of view. He wishes to deny the reality of evil and to create a harmonistic outlook on life. The result of such an experience is bitter disappointment. Evil mocks the prisoner of fate and his fantasy of a reality that is all good and pleasant.

However, in the realm of destiny man recognizes reality as it is, and does not desire to use harmonizing formulas in order to hide and disregard evil. The "Child of Destiny" is very realistic and does not flinch in anticipation of a face-to-face confrontation with evil. His approach is halakhic[B] and moral, and thus devoid of any metaphysical/speculative nuance. When the "Child of Destiny" suffers, he says in his heart, "There is evil, I do not deny it, and I will not conceal it with fruitless casuistry. I am, however, interested in it from a halakhic point of view; and as a person who wants to know what action to take. I ask a single question: What should the sufferer do to live with his suffering?" In this dimension, the emphasis is removed *from* causal and teleological considerations (which differ only as to direction) and is directed *to* the realm of action. The problem is now formulated in the language of a simple halakhah and revolves around a quotidian (i.e. daily) task. The question

---

[B] That is, in accordance with traditional Jewish law.

of questions is: What does suffering obligate man to do? This problem was important to Judaism, which placed it at the center of its *Weltanschauung*. Halakhah is just as interested in this question, as in issues of *issur*[C] and *heter*[D] and *hiyyuv*[E] and *p'tur*.[F] We do not wonder about the ineffable ways of the Holy One, but instead ponder the paths man must take when evil leaps up at him. We ask not about the reason for evil and its purpose, but rather about its rectification and uplifting. How should a man react in a time of distress? What should a person do so as not to rot in his affliction?

The halakhic answer to this question is very simple. Suffering comes to elevate man, to purify his spirit and sanctify him, to cleanse his mind and purify it from the chaff of superficiality and the dross of crudeness; to sensitize his soul and expand his horizons. In general, the purpose of suffering is to repair the imperfection in man's persona. The halakhah teaches us that an afflicted person commits a criminal act if he allows his pain to go for naught and to remain without meaning or purpose. Suffering appears in the world in order to contribute something to man, in order to atone for him, in order to redeem him from moral impurity, from crudeness and lowliness of spirit. The sufferer must arise therefrom, purified, refined, and cleansed. "An hour of

---

[C] Prohibitions.

[D] Lit. "permission." That which is permitted under Jewish law.

[E] Obligation under Jewish law.

[F] Exemption under Jewish law.

distress it is for Jacob, and from it he should be saved"
(Jeremiah 30:7). From the midst of suffering itself he
will achieve lasting redemption and merit a self-actual-
ization and exaltation that are unequaled in a world
devoid of suffering. From negation sprouts affirmation;
from antithesis, thesis emerges; and from a denial of
existence, a new existence is revealed. The Torah gave
witness to man's mighty spiritual reaction to suffering
inflicted upon him when it said, "In your distress when
all these horrors shall come upon you .... then you shall
return to the Lord your God" (Deuteronomy 4:30).
Suffering requires man to repent and return to God.[3]
Distress is designated to arouse us to repentance, and
what is repentance if not the renewal and supreme
redemption of man?

How pitiful if man's sufferings do not bring him to a
spiritual crisis, and his soul remains frozen and bereft of
forgiveness. How pitiful is the sufferer if his soul is not
warmed by the flame of suffering, and if his wounds do
not spark "the Candle of God" (Proverbs 20:27) within
him. When pain wanders in the wide world as a blind
force without purpose, a stinging indictment of the man
who squanders his suffering issues forth.

Judaism made this notion more profound when it
combined the idea of the repair (*tikkun*)[G] of evil and its

---

[G] The concept of *tikkun*, drawn from the Kabbalah, is the doctrine
of the restoration of unity and harmony in the universe after the
metaphysical fissure that occurred in the course of Creation.

elevation with the perfection and elevation of goodness.
Judaism states that the kindnesses of God are not given
to man as an unconditional gift, without obligation; they
require something in return; their very essence imposes
a moral, halakhic demand upon the man who enjoys
them. Indeed, while loving-kindness emanates from the
open, overflowing, generous hand of the Holy One, it is
not an unlimited or unconditional gift. Such a gift is not
absolute. The bestowing of good is always conditional
and temporary. When God bestows wealth, property,
influence, and honor, the recipient must know how to
employ them; how to turn these precious gifts into fruitful, creative powers, how to include others in his happiness and greatness, and how to render loving-kindness
with the divine kindnesses that emanate and issue forth
to him from a never-ending font. If an abundance of
good does not bring man to absolute subordination to
the Holy One, then he is guilty of a fundamental sin
resulting in the severe distress that in turn reminds him
of his obligation to the Creator of the universe for the
gift of His kindnesses. Our great sages have taught: "Man
is obligated to give thanks for evil as he does for goodness" (M. Berakhot 9:5). Just as good obliges man to perform deeds of a higher order and demands creative and
innovative actions from the individual or the populace,
so does suffering require the repair of the soul and the
cleansing of life — if at the time of God's favor and
beneficence one was not aroused to action. For it hap-
pens that man is summoned to repair, through his afflic-

tions, the damage he caused in God's creation at the hour when the Holy One extended His bounty. The feeling of subordination to the Almighty and the understanding of one's obligation to purify and sanctify one's self by dint of one's suffering must brighten man's soul when he finds himself in distress and perplexed by his existence. He must overcome the obtuseness of his heart that caused him to sin when he stood in the presence of God's bounty. In short, man must solve, not the question of the causal or teleological reason for suffering with all its speculative complexity, but rather the question of its curative role, in all its halakhic simplicity, by turning fate to destiny and elevating himself from object to subject, from thing to man.

Chapter 2
Job

Indeed! This is the answer that was given by the Creator to Job. As long as Job, as a slave of fate, philosophized about reasons, and motives, and demanded insight into the essence of evil, continually asking and murmuring: "Why and wherefore does suffering come," the Holy One answered him sharply with the pointed question: "Did you know?" (Job 39:1).

> [Did you know] [w]ho it is who darkens counsel by speaking words without knowledge? Gird up now your loins like a man, for I will demand of you and you shall declare unto Me. Where were you when I laid the foundations of the earth? Declare if you have such understanding. . . . Do you know the time when the wild goats of the rock will give birth; when the hinds will calve?
> —Job 38:2-4, 39:1

If you do not know the alphabet of creation, why be so impudent as to ask questions about the workings of the world? But once Job realized how strange his question was and how great his ignorance, and acknowledged it and was not ashamed to say: "[T]herefore I have uttered that which I did not understand; things too wonderful for me which I know not" (Job 42:3), then God was able to reveal to this man of destiny the true principles which are concealed in suffering, as expressed by the halakhah. The Holy One said: Job! True, you will never understand the inner essence of the why, the reason for suffering and its purpose, but there is one thing that you are obligated to know: the basis for the repair of suffering. If by your suffering you are able to elevate yourself to the spiritual level that you have not heretofore attained, you will then know that your travail was intended as a device for your perfection in both spirit and soul. Job! When My graciousness engulfed you in the manner expressed by the prophet, "Behold, I will extend prosperity to [him] a like a river" (Isaiah 66:12) and you were well known and a man of influence ("And this man was the greatest of all the children of the East" [Job 1:3]), you did not fulfill the role that My grace placed upon you. You were a sound and just man, God-fearing and avoiding of evil. You did not use your power and wealth for ill. You gave much charity ("Righteousness I wore, and it robed me, my justice was a robe and turban" [Job 29:14]). You did not hesitate to offer assistance and support to others, and you stood by them in their hour of peril and distress ("Did I not deliver the poor that cried out and the orphaned that had none to help him?" [Job 29:12]). However, you were still short of attaining that great trait of loving-kindness in two respects: (a) never did you bear the communal yoke, nor did you participate in the trouble and grief of the community,[A] and (b) you did not feel the pain of [i.e., empathize with] the individual sufferer. As a man blessed with a good heart, you may have momentarily pitied the orphan. You had vast amounts of money and you wanted for nothing, hence you gave a respectable amount of tzedakah [charity]. However, loving-kindness encompasses more than fleeting sentiment and cheap sentimentality. Loving-kindness demands more than a momentary tear and a cold coin.[B] Loving-kindness means empathizing with one's fellow man, identifying with his hurt and feeling responsibility for his fate. You did not possess this attribute of overflowing loving-kindness [in imitation of the Creator], neither in your public nor in your personal relationships.

You were a contemporary of Jacob[4], who wrestled with Laban, Esau, and the angel at the stream of Yabok (Genesis 32:23–32). Did you help Jacob with advice? Who was Jacob? A poor shepherd. And you? You were rich and a man of influence. Had you related to Jacob with appropriate sympathy and with steadfast loving-kindness, he would not have had to pass through such a multitude of tribulations.

You lived in the time of Moses, and you were numbered among the advisers of Pharaoh. Did you lift a fin-

---

[A] TB Bava Batra 15b.
[B] TB Bava Batra 15b, Megillah 28a.

ger when Pharaoh issued his evil decree that "Every son that is born you shall cast into the river" (Exodus 1:22), or when the oppressors enslaved your brethren with back-breaking work? You were silent then and did not protest, for you were afraid of identifying yourself with the unfortunate slaves.[C] To toss them a coin? Yes; but to publicly demonstrate for them? No! You were afraid that you would be accused of dual-loyalty.

You were active in the generation of Ezra and Nehemiah, the returnees to Zion. You, Job, with your wealth and influence, could have hastened the process of settling the Land of Israel and rebuilding the Temple. However, your ear was deafened and did not heed the historical cries of the nation.

You did not storm out in protest against the Sanballites, the Samaritans, and the rest of Israel's enemies who wanted to destroy the *Yishuv*[D] and extinguish the spark of the last hope of God's people. What did you do in the hour when the returnees from the Diaspora cried out from the depths of suffering and despair: "The

---

[C] TB Sotah 11a:" R. Hiya the son of R. Abba said in the name of R. Simai: There were three people in Pharaoh's company [when he took counsel as to how to deal with the people of Israel]: Balaam, Job and Jethro. Balaam, who gave the advice [that Pharaoh took], was punished by death (he died in war with the Medes). Job, who was silent, was punished with afflictions. Jethro, who ran away [and did not want to participate in this evil counsel], was privileged to see his later generations sit in the judgment chamber in the Temple . . . ."

[D] The community of Israel as rebuilt by Ezra and Nehemiah *circa* 400 B.C.E.

strength of the bearers of the burdens has faltered and there is much rubbish, so that we are not able to build the wall" (Nehemiah 4:4)? You sat with folded arms! You did not participate in the travail of those who fought for Judaism, for Israel, and the redemption. Never did you bring even one sacrifice on their behalf. All these years you worried only about your own welfare and only for your own benefit did you pray and offer sacrifices:

> And so it was when the days of their feasting were over, that Job sent word to his children to sanctify themselves and he [Job] rose up early in the morning, and offered burnt offerings for each of them all, for Job said: "It may be that my sons have sinned, and blasphemed God in their hearts."
>
> —Job 1:5

Did you once, Job, participate in a stranger's grief to the extent of making a plea on his behalf? No, you did not![E] Do you know, Job, that prayer is the province of the community, and that an individual does not come before the Lord to plead before Him and request the fulfillment of his needs until he redeems himself from isolation and self-containment and joins the community? Did you forget that Jewish prayer speaks in the plural ("One should

---

[E] TB Sotah 11a.

always join together with the community in prayer" [TB Berakhot 3a]), and that Jewish prayer is the linking of one soul to another and the fusing of tempestuous hearts. You did not know how to use the formula for prayer fixed by the nation, which is to include yourself within the community and to help bear the burden of one's fellow man. If your soul wants to comprehend the doctrine of the amelioration of suffering, you must grasp the secret of prayer that brings the "I" close to the other. The original formula that joins the individual with the experience of the community must become for you second nature; and you must understand the idea of loving-kindness, which is realized by the one who prays and who is elevated from a personal self-concern to becoming one with the community. You will not fulfill your obligation by generously dispensing the miserable pennies with which you were blessed. You will only be saved through prayer resulting from the experience of communal travail. You did not understand the teaching of *hesed*,[F] and you squandered My blessings. Try now to comprehend the lesson of suffering. Perhaps, out of pain and grief, you can undo the errors you committed out of illusory comfort and happiness.

The Holy One said to the friends of Job, "Now, therefore, take unto you seven bullocks and seven rams, and go to My servant Job and offer up for yourselves a burnt-offering, and My servant Job shall pray for you" (Job

---

[F] Acts of loving-kindness.

42:8). Behold, I will test Job yet another time. Let him be tested publicly. Does he now know how to pray for others and participate in their travail? Did he learn anything in the hour of retribution and divine anger? Did he adopt for himself a new style of collective prayer that encompasses the community? If he pleads for you, he will bring his salvation and yours; "For to him I will show favor" (Job 42:8). Then you shall know that Job was redeemed from the narrow straits of egotism and entered into the vistas of communal empathy; and that social isolation has ended and communal affiliation has appeared in its stead. A wonderful thing happened. Job suddenly understood the nature of Jewish prayer. He discovered in one moment its plural voice and the attribute of loving-kindness that sweeps man from the private to the public domain. He began to live a communal life, to feel the community's hurts, to mourn its disasters and rejoice in its moments of celebration. Job's sufferings found their true repair in his escape from the prison in which he had found himself, and God's wrath was assuaged. As it is written: "And the Lord changed the fortunes of Job *when he prayed for his friends*" (Job 42:10).

Chapter 3
Missing the Appointed Hour

We too are living in troubled times, in days of anger and distress. We have been afflicted with violent pogroms and have become accustomed to suffering. In the past fifteen years [1941-56] we have undergone tortuous ordeals that are unparalleled in thousands of years of diaspora, degradation, and destruction. This chapter of suffering did not end with the establishment of the State of Israel. To this day the State is still in a condition of crisis and danger, and we all fear for its future. We are all eye-witnesses to the rising star of the iniquitous and to the corruption of international law by the Western nations out of indifference to the principles of justice and fairness. All try to curry favor with our enemies and bow and scrape before them with false humility and shameful hypocrisy. All are concerned with the welfare of our enemies, and remain indifferent to the suffering Jewish State (much like the rich man who stole the lamb of his poor, powerless, and uninfluential neighbor [II Samuel 12:1-6]).

The well-known metaphysical query surfaces and the sufferer asks: "Why do you show me iniquity and cause [us] to behold mischief. . . for the wicked man

besets the righteous, so that justice goes out perverted?"
(Habakkuk 1:3–4). Indeed, as we emphasized above, God
does not address this question, and it is not answered. It
remains hidden, beyond the realm of logic. For "you cannot see My face, for man may not see Me and live"
(Exodus 33:20). When the desire for rational inquiry
seizes man, he can do nothing but fortify his belief in the
Creator, accept God's judgment, and acknowledge the
perfection of His action. "He is the Rock, His works are
perfect: for all His ways are just" (Deuteronomy 32:4). If
we want to ask a penetrating question at a time beset by
terrifying nightmares, it is incumbent upon us to do so in
a halakhic mode: What obligation accrues to the sufferer
as a result of his suffering? What commanding heavenly
voice breaks through from the midst of suffering? As we
have said, this question has a solution which is expressed
in a simple halakhah. There is no need for metaphysical
speculation in order to clarify the rules of rectifying evil.
"For it is not in Heaven" (Deuteronomy 30:12). If we succeed in formulating this doctrine without dealing with
questions of cause and telos, we will earn a complete salvation, and the scriptural promise will be fulfilled for us,
as it is written: "Take counsel together, and it shall come
to naught; speak your harshnesses and they shall not
come to fruition, for God is with us" (Isaiah 8:10). Then
and only then shall we emerge from the depths of the
Holocaust with enhanced spiritual stature and augment-
ed historical splendor, as it is written, "And the Lord gave
Job twice as much as he had before" (Job 42:10) — dou-
ble in quantity and quality.

When the doctrine of the corrective effect of suffering is put into practice, it demands of the sufferer
courage and spiritual discipline. He must gird himself
with extraordinary strength, make a detached assess-
ment of his world, examine his past and look to his
future with complete honesty. The lesson of Job's suffering did not come to him easily. And we, too, who are soft-
hearted, weak-willed, bound by fate, and devoid of spiritual strength, are now bidden by Providence to adopt a
new attitude; to ascend and raise ourselves to a level
where suffering teaches us to demand from ourselves
redemption and deliverance. For this purpose we must
look at our reflection with spiritual fortitude and pure
objectivity. This reflection bursts through to us from
both the present and the past.

If God's grace, which is given to either an individual
or a community, requires certain actions of the beneficiary, even if the gifts (such as wealth, honor, influence,
power, etc., which are attained by exhausting effort) are
granted to man by natural means, how much more so is
it true that Divine gifts given supernaturally, in the form
of miracles that transcend the framework of the elementary laws of historical causality, must subject the
recipient of the miracles to God. Miraculous grace places
upon man an absolute responsibility to fulfill the larger
imperative that calls out from the miracle. A transcen-
dental imperative always accompanies miraculous activity. "Command the Children of Israel" (e.g., Numbers 5:2,
28:1, 34:2, 35:2). Woe unto the beneficiary of a miracle
who does not recognize it for what it is, and whose ear

is deaf to the echo of the imperative that arises out of this metahistorical event. Pity the one who benefits from the miracles of the Master of the Universe but the spark of faith is not kindled in him, and his conscience is not stirred by the sight of this singular event.

When a miracle does not find its appropriate echo in actual deeds, a lofty vision dissipates and is squandered, whereupon Divine Justice indicts the ungrateful recipient of the miracle. "The Holy One sought to make Hezekiah the Messiah and Sennacherib, Gog of Armageddon. However, God's Justice said to Him . . . 'Hezekiah, for whom You wrought all these miracles, did not sing in praise before You. Shall You make him Messiah?'".[5] Then comes distress, the hour of misery. Suffering is the final warning given by Providence to the man, who is devoid of gratitude for the good God has done for him. To the final proclamation that issues forth from suffering, one must react quickly and answer the call of the Almighty, who cries out to him, "Where are you?" (Genesis 3:9). Judaism has been very careful about not missing the appointed hour. It has a very sensitive time awareness; any delay is considered sinful. Man may sometimes lose his entire world for but one sin — that of tarrying. "But he lingered" (Genesis 19:16). What is the sin of leaving over a sacrifice, if not missing the appointed hour (Leviticus 19:5-8)? What is the desecration of the Sabbath, if not the performing of prohibited actions one second after the setting of the sun — work that just one second before was permitted? How does the loss of the ability to perform a *mitzvah*[A] occur if not for the tarrying of a few moments, such as reciting the passages of the *Shema*[B] after its appointed hour or the taking of the *Lulav* and *Etrog*[C] after sunset, and the like? Two kings of Israel, both equally the anointed of the Lord and heroes of the nation, sinned, repented fully, and confessed. One God did not absolve; the other was immediately forgiven upon his confession. With regard to Saul, God acted in accordance with the demands of strict justice and tore the kingdom from him. With respect to David, He tempered justice with mercy and his dynasty was not wrested from his children. Why was the Holy One so strict with Saul and compassionate with David? The question does not require special analysis. The answer is quite simple. David did not miss the opportunity and immediately confessed his sin; Saul tarried a bit, and for this delay kingship was wrested from him. When Nathan the prophet came to David and uttered his cry, "You are the man!" (II Samuel 12:7), David, in the blinking of an eye, began his confession. "And David said to Nathan, I have

---

[A] Plural *Mitzvot*, Commandments (injunctions both positive and negative) which Jews must fulfill; 613 of which arise from the Bible and seven of which are of rabbinic origin.

[B] The proclamation of God's unity consisting of three portions of the Pentateuch: Deuteronomy 6:4-9; Deuteronomy 11:13-21; and Numbers 15:37-41

[C] The palm branch and the citron (a citrus fruit) two of the Four Species which are held on the Jewish festival of Tabernacles (*Sukkot*). Leviticus 33:40.

sinned against the Lord" (II Samuel 12:13). After he heard Samuel's reprimand, Saul wasted one precious second, a second "more precious than gold and pearls" (Proverbs 20:15). "And why did you not listen to the command of God but instead went after the booty?" (I Samuel 15:19). Saul began to argue with the prophet and only later confessed: "And Saul [initially] said to Samuel: 'Indeed I have done what God has commanded me to do, and I have gone along the path in which the Lord has sent me'" (I Samuel 15:20). Indeed, in that confrontation, [after a moment's reflection] he also confessed his sins out of a broken heart and a tempest-tossed spirit. "And Saul said . . . 'I have sinned, for I transgressed God's command and your instructions'" (I Samuel 15:24). But this confession was not timely, and a momentary lag such as this caused Saul to lose his kingdom. By the time Saul confessed, the decree was already sealed and the opportunity was lost. "The Lord has rent the kingdom of Israel from you" (I Samuel 15:28). If Saul had not missed the proper moment, and had he not been among the laggards, his dynasty would have continued.[6]

What is the essence the story of the Song of Songs, if not the description of a paradoxical and tragic hesitation on the part of the love-intoxicated, anxiety-stricken Lover, when the opportunity, couched in majestic awe, presented itself? What is it, if not the deferral of a great and sublime opportunity pregnant with a possibility of which she dreamed, for which she fought, which she sought, and for which she had searched with all the fervor of her soul? The delicate and refined Lover, passion-driven to her fair-eyed Beloved, who in days resplendent in brightness wandered the paths of the vineyards, the mountain ridges, through wheat fields and orchards, and in evenings bathed in the pale light of an enchanting moon or gloomy with darkness passed between the walls in search of her Lover — she returned one rain-stormy night to her tent, tired and weary, and fell asleep. The patter of quick-moving, light footsteps was heard in the stillness of the tent. In that mysterious and strange night, the Beloved for whom she had so hoped and kept watch, suddenly appeared out of the darkness and beckoned at the entrance of her tent. He knocked and pleaded that she open the door for Him.[D] "Listen! My Beloved Is Knocking,[E] saying, 'Open to me, my sister, my love, my dove, my undefiled: for my head is drenched with dew, and my locks with the damp of the night'" (Song of Songs 5:2). The great moment for which she had been waiting with such longing came at a time of inattentiveness. The elusive and secretive Beloved, weary of wandering and tribulations, appeared with His curly locks, black eyes, powerful build, and shining countenance. He stood in her doorway and thrust His hand through the hole in the lock, seeking shelter from the

---

[D] The allegorical interpretation of the Song of Songs provides that the "Beloved" refers to the Almighty and thus the pronouns "him, his, and he" will be written with a capital "H".

[E] Song of Songs 5:2. The translation is per Ibn Ezra, Genesis, 4:10, s.v. *tzoakim eilai*.

dampness of the night. He wanted to recount to her His mighty love, His longing and yearning for a life together filled with desire and joy, and of fulfillment of expectations and realization of dreams. A simple extension of the hand to turn the lock separated the Lover and her Beloved — the great dream from its complete fulfillment. With one leap the Lover could have attained all her life's desires. "Draw me, we will run after you. . . . We will be glad and rejoice in you" (Song of Songs 1:4). Deceitful is the heart (Jeremiah 17:9), however, and who can explain it? That very night, sloth, the result of a strange inertia, took hold of the Lover. For one small moment the flame of yearning that burned within her was buried, the mighty desire withered, and her feelings and dreams were silenced. The Lover refused to leave her bed. She did not open the door of her tent to her handsome Beloved. A cruel confusion swept her into forgetfulness and apathy. The Lover became lazy and stubborn, she poured forth countless excuses and pretexts to explain her strange behavior. "I have removed my cloak, how shall I put it on again? I have washed my feet, how shall I soil them?" (Song of Songs 5:3). The Beloved continued to beckon, and as His beckoning became more persistent, so too did the insanity that chilled and tainted the Lover.

So long as the whispering of the Beloved split the hush of the night, so did the heart of the Lover harden. Pleading and patient the Beloved continued to beckon while the minutes and hours of the clock were ticking away. The Lover did not respond to the voice of the Beloved. The door to her tent was locked shut. The opportunity was lost, and the vision of an exalted life died. True, after a brief delay the Lover awoke from her slumber and jumped in haste from her bed to greet the Beloved. "I rose up to open to my Beloved" (Song of Songs 5:5), but the leap came too late. The Beloved had stopped beckoning and had disappeared into the darkness of the night, "My Beloved had turned away, and was gone" (Song of Songs 5:6). The joy of her life was exiled. Her existence became a desert, a storehouse of emptiness. The episodes of feverish search returned. She, the Lover, still wanders through the dwellings of the shepherds seeking her Beloved.

Chapter 4
Six Knocks

Eight years ago, in the midst of a night of the terrors of Majdanek, Treblinka, and Buchenwald; in a night of gas chambers and crematoria; in a night of total divine self-concealment; in a night ruled by the devil of doubt and destruction who sought to sweep the Lover from her own tent into the Catholic Church; in a night of continuous searching for the Beloved — on that very night the Beloved appeared. The Almighty, who was hiding in His splendid *sanctum*, suddenly appeared and began to beckon at the tent of the Lover, who tossed and turned on her bed beset by convulsions and the agonies of hell. Because of the beating and knocking at the door of the mournful Lover, the State of Israel was born.

How many times did the Beloved knock on the door of the Lover? It appears to me that we can count at least six knocks.

First, the knock of the Beloved was heard in the political arena. From the point of view of international relations, no one will deny that the rebirth of the State of Israel, in a political sense, was an almost supernatural occurrence. Both Russia and the Western nations supported the establishment of the State of Israel. This was

perhaps the one resolution on which East and West con-
curred [during the Cold War era]. I am inclined to
believe that the United Nations was especially created
for this end — for the sake of fulfilling the mission that
Divine Providence had placed upon it. It appears to me
that one cannot point to any other concrete accomplishment on the part of the United Nations. Our Rabbis
of blessed memory already expressed this view: At times
rain falls on account of one individual and for one blade
of grass (Breishit Rabbah 66:2). I do not know who the
representatives of the press, with their human eyes, saw
to be the chairman in that fateful session of the General
Assembly in which the creation of the State of Israel was
decided, but he who looked carefully with his spiritual
eye saw the true Chairman who conducted the pro-
ceedings — the Beloved. He knocked with his gavel on
the lectern. Do we not interpret the passage "On that
night the *king* could not sleep" (Esther 6:1) as meaning
the that the *King of the Universe* could not sleep? If
Ahasuerus alone had been sleepless, the matter would
not have been at all important and salvation would not
have arisen on that night. If, however, the King, the
Master of the Universe, could not sleep, as it were,
redemption would be born. If just anyone were to have
opened the session of the United Nations, the State of
Israel would not have been born. But it was the Beloved
who rapped on the Chairman's lectern, and the miracle
materialized. Listen! My Beloved Knocks!

Second, the knock of the Beloved was heard on the battlefield. The tiny defense forces of [the State of] Israel defeated the mighty Arab armies. The miracle of "the many delivered into the hands of the few"[A] materialized before our eyes, and an even greater miracle happened! God hardened the heart of Ishmael and commanded him to go into battle against the State of Israel. Had the Arabs not declared war on Israel and instead supported the Partition Plan, the State of Israel would have remained without Jerusalem, without a major portion of the Galilee, and without some areas of the Negev. If thousands of years ago Pharaoh had allowed the children of Israel to leave immediately, as Moses had originally requested, Moses would have been bound by his word to return in three days. Pharaoh, however, hardened his heart and did not listen to Moses. "The Holy One then took Israel out with a mighty hand and by an outstretched arm" (Deuteronomy 4:34). Consequently, the force of the promise [that the children of Israel would return to Egypt] was vitiated. No contract that is based upon mutuality of promise binds one side if the other party refuses to fulfill its obligations. Listen! My Beloved Knocks!

Third, the Beloved also began to knock on the door of the tent of theology, and possibly this is the strongest beckoning. I have, on several occasions, emphasized in my remarks concerning the Land of Israel that the theo-

---

[A] From the special addition to the Amidah recited on Chanukkah.

logical arguments of Christian theologians to the effect
that the Holy One has taken away from the Community
of Israel its rights to the Land of Israel, and that all of the
biblical promises relating to Zion and Jerusalem now
refer in an allegorical sense to Christianity and the
Christian Church, were all publicly shown to be false,
baseless contentions by the establishment of the State of
Israel. One must have a broad familiarity with theologi-
cal literature from the time of Justin Martyr[B] down to the
theologians of our own day to comprehend the full
extent of this marvel by which the central axiom of
Christian theology was shattered. We should pay careful
attention to the learned explanation of our Secretary of
State, Mr. Dulles (who served as the deacon of an
Episcopalian Church), to a Committee of the United
States Senate that the Arabs hate the Jews because they
killed the founder of their religion. This "explanation"
possesses hidden and deep symbolic significance. I am
not a psychiatrist and surely not a psychoanalyst, but I
know how to study Talmud, and I remember well what
our Rabbis of blessed memory said about Balaam: "from
his blessings . . . you may learn what was in his heart" (TB
Sanhedrin 105b). Sometimes, when a person speaks too
much, something of the truth slips out. When one of the

[B] Justin Martyr, (*ca.* 100–165 C.E.), the author of one of the earliest
anti-Jewish polemical tracts by a Christian theologian. See e.g.
Dialogue with Trypho (the Jew) wherin Martyr tries to demonstrate
that a New Covenant has superseded the old Covenant of God with
the Jewish people and that the gentiles have been selected to
replace Israel as God's chosen people.

Senators asked the Secretary of State, "Why do the Arabs hate the Jews?" he really wanted to answer, "Personally, I too, as a Christian, have no great love for them, because they killed our messiah and consequently forfeited their portion of Abraham's heritage." An angel sat in the throat of the Secretary, or a hook was put into it (as in the exegesis of the Rabbis of blessed memory on the phrase "and God put a word in Balaam's mouth" [Numbers 23:5, TB Sotah 10a], "[i.e.] he put a hook in his mouth"), and instead of saying, "Our Lord" and "for myself," he let other words slip out, the "Arabs" and "Mohammed." In his subconscious he was terrified of the "awful" fact that the Community of Israel rules over Zion and Jerusalem. I find satisfaction in reading about the State of Israel in the Catholic and Protestant newspapers. Despite themselves they must mention the name of Israel when they report the news of Zion and Jerusalem, which we possess. I always have a special sense of satisfaction when I read in the paper that Israel's reaction is not as yet known because today is Saturday and government offices are closed or when I read, on the eve of Passover, an item from the United Press that "Jews will sit down tonight to the seder table in the hope that the miracles of Egypt will return and recur today." Listen! My Beloved Knocks!

Fourth, the Beloved knocks in the heart of the youth which is assimilated and perplexed. The period of *hester panim*[C] in the 1940's brought confusion among the

---

[C] *Lit.* The "hiding of countenance." This is the notion of the removal of Divine protection from the Jewish people.

Jewish masses and especially Jewish youth. Assimilation increased, and the urge to flee from Judaism and the Jewish people reached its apex. Fear, despair, and ignorance caused many to forsake the Jewish community and "climb aboard the ship," to flee to Tarshish from the presence of the Lord (Jonah 1:3), just as Jonah sought to flee God's presence. A seemingly unstoppable tidal wave stood over us and threatened to destroy us. Suddenly, the Beloved began to beckon to the hearts of the perplexed, and His beckoning, the establishment of the State of Israel, at least slowed the process of flight. Many who were once alienated are now bound to the Jewish State with ties of pride in its mighty accomplishments. Many American Jews who were partially assimilated find themselves beset by hidden fear and concern for any crisis that the State of Israel is at the time passing through, and they pray for its well-being and welfare even though they are far from being totally committed to it. Even Jews who are hostile to the State of Israel must defend themselves from the strange charge of dual-loyalty and proclaim daily and declare that they have no stake in the Holy Land. It is good for a Jew when he cannot ignore his Jewishness and is obliged to perpetually answer the questions "Who are you?" and "What is your occupation?" (Jonah 1:8), even when extraordinary fear grips him and he does not have the strength or fortitude to answer with true pride, "I am a Jew, and I fear the Lord, the God of heaven" (Jonah 1:9). The unrelenting question of, "Who are you?" ties him to the Jewish people.

The very mention of the name Israel is a reminder to the fleeing Jew that he cannot escape from the community of Israel in whose midst he has been enmeshed from birth. Everywhere we turn we hear the name "Israel." When we listen to a radio station, when we open a paper, when we participate in a debate on current events, we encounter the question of Israel; it is always a topic of public concern.

This phenomenon is extremely important for Jews who are afflicted with self-hatred and want to turn away from Judaism and run for their lives. They hide, like Jonah in his day, in the recesses of the ship (Jonah 1:5) and seek to "slumber" (Jonah 1:5). The Captain, however, does not permit them to ignore their fate. The shadow of Israel continuously chases after them. Random thoughts and paradoxical reflections arise from the subconscious of even the most confirmed assimilationist. And when a Jew begins to think, to reflect, when he is unable to sleep, it is impossible to know where his thoughts will take him and how his doubts will be expressed. Listen! My Beloved Knocks!

The fifth knock of the Beloved is perhaps the most important. For the first time in the annals of our exile, Divine Providence has amazed our enemies with the astounding discovery that Jewish blood is not cheap! If the antisemites describe this phenomenon as being "an eye for an eye," we will agree with them. If we want to courageously defend our continued national and historical existence, we must, from time to time, interpret the verse of an "eye for an eye" literally. So many "eyes" were lost in the course of our bitter exile because we did *not* repay hurt for hurt. The time has come for us to fulfill the simple meaning of "an eye for an eye." (Exodus 21:24) Of course, I am sure everyone recognizes that I am an adherent of the Oral Law, and from my perspective there is no doubt that the verse refers to monetary restitution, as defined by halakhah. However, with respect to the Mufti[D] and Nasser,[E] I would demand that we interpret the verse in accordance with its literal meaning — the taking of an actual eye! Pay no attention to the saccharine suggestions of known assimilationists and of some Jewish socialists who stand pat in their rebelliousness and think they are still living in Bialystok, Brest-Litovsk, and Minsk of the year 1905,[F] and openly declare that revenge is forbidden to the Jewish people in any place, at any time, and under all circumstances. "Vanity of vanities!" (Ecclesiastes 1:2) Revenge is forbidden when it is

---

[D] Haj Amin Al-Husseini (1897-1974), who dominated the Arab nationalist movement in Palestine and led the anti-Jewish riots in 1921, 1929, and 1936. The Mufti collaborated with Hitler and led the Nazi coup in Iraq during World War II. Prior to the invasion by five Arab armies in May, 1948, he led the armed opposition to the future State of Israel.

[E] Gammal Abdel Nasser (1918-1970), Prime Minister of Egypt (1954-1956), President 1956-1970, led Egypt during the Suez Campaign (1956) and the Six-Day War (1967).

[F] Russian cities where the Black Hundreds carried out pogroms against the Jews in 1905, accusing them of sympathy for the Japanese during the Russo-Japanese War.

pointless, but if one is aroused thereby to self-defense, it is the most elementary right of man to take his revenge.

The Torah has always taught that a man is permitted, indeed, has a sacred obligation, to defend himself. With the verse, "If a burglar is caught in the act of breaking in" (Exodus 22:1), the Torah establishes the halakhah that one may defend not only one's life but his property as well.[7] If the thief who comes to take the property of the householder is capable of killing the householder (should the householder not comply with his demands), the householder may rise up against the criminal and kill him. For good reason the Torah relates that two of its great heroes, Abraham and Moses, took sword in hand to defend their brethren: "And when Abraham heard that his kinsman was taken captive, he led forth his retainers" (Genesis 14:14). "And when Moses saw the Egyptian smite a Jew . . . he struck down the Egyptian" (Exodus 2:11–12). This behavior does not contradict the principle of loving-kindness and compassion. On the contrary, a passive position, without self-defense, may sometimes lead to the most awesome brutality. "And I will gain honor from Pharaoh, and all his hosts, his chariots, and his horsemen. And the Egyptians will know that I am the Lord" (Exodus 14:17–18). God did not seek honor and recognition. He wanted Pharaoh, Moses' contemporary, to know that he must pay a high price for his edict that "Every male child born shall be cast into the river" (Exodus 1:22). His present desire is that the blood of Jewish children who were slain as they recited the eighteen benedictions of the daily [Amidah] prayer shall also be avenged. When God smote the Egyptians, He sought to demonstrate that there will always be accountability for the spilling of Jewish blood. At present, it is necessary not only to convince the dictator of Egypt [Nasser], but the self-righteous Nehru,[G] the Foreign Office in London, and the sanctimonious members of the United Nations, that Jewish blood is not cheap. Therefore, how laughable it is when they try to persuade us to rely on the declaration of the three Great Powers guaranteeing the status quo.[H] We all know from experience what value can be attached to the pronouncements of the British Foreign Office and the so-called friendship of certain officials in our State Department. In general, how absurd is the request that an entire people be dependent on the kindnesses of others and remain without the ability to defend itself. Public and private honor is dependent upon the possibility of defending one's life and one's honor. A people that cannot defend its freedom and tranquility is neither free nor independent. The third of the

---

[G] Jawaharlal Nehru (1889–1964), Prime Minister of the Republic of India from 1947 to 1964.

[H] Declaration of the United States, Britain, and France warning that "Should the three Governments . . . find any one of these states [Israel or its Arab neighbors] contemplates violating the frontiers of the armistice lines they will . . . act both within and without the framework of the United Nations to prevent such a violation." Howard M. Sachar, *A History of Israel* (New York: Alfred A. Knopf, New York, 1982), p. 458.

phrases of Divine redemption is "And I shall redeem you with an outstretched hand and with great judgments" (Exodus 6:6). Thank God we have lived to see the day when, with the help of God, Jews have it within their power to defend themselves.

Let us not forget that the poison of Hitlerite anti-semitism (which made Jews fair game to all) still permeates this generation, which looked with equanimity upon the horrible scene of the suffocation of millions in gas chambers as a normal event that need not be challenged. The antidote for this venom that poisoned minds and dulled hearts is the readiness of the State of Israel to defend the lives of its citizens. Listen! My Beloved Knocks!

The sixth beckoning, of which we should also not lose sight, was heard at the time of the opening of the gates of the Land of Israel. A Jew escaping from an enemy's land now knows that he can find refuge in the land of his forefathers. This is a new phenomenon in the annals of our history. Up to now, when a Jewish population was uprooted, it wandered in the wilderness of the nations without finding shelter and habitation. The shutting of the gates in the face of the exiled caused total destruction for much of the Jewish people. Now the situation has changed. When any nation expels its Jewish minority, the exiled now direct their steps to Zion, and she, as a compassionate mother, absorbs them. We are all witnesses to the settlement of Oriental Jewry in Israel over the last several years. Who knows what would have been in store for these brothers of ours in the lands of their origin if not for the State of Israel, which brought them to her in planes and ships? Had Israel been born before the Hitlerian Holocaust, hundreds of thousands of Jews could have been saved from the gas chambers and the crematoria. The miracle of the State tarried somewhat, and in the wake of its delay, thousands and tens of thousands of Jews were taken to the slaughter. Now that the hour of *hester panim*[1] has passed, however, the possibility exists for Jews who are pried from their homes to take root in the Holy Land. This should not be taken lightly. Listen! My Beloved Knocks!

---

[1] See Note C this section.

Chapter 5
The Obligation of Torah Judaism
to the Land of Israel

What was our reaction to the beckoning of the voice of the Beloved, to the munificence of His loving-kindness and miracles? Did we get out of our beds and immediately open the door, or did we continue to rest like the Lover [in the story of the Song of Songs], and were we too lazy to get out of our beds? "I have washed my feet, how shall I soil them?" (Song of Songs 5:3).

All the trembling and fear for the geographical integrity of the State of Israel, all the suggestions of our enemies which are directed at territorial concessions by the State of Israel, and all of the brazen demands of the Arabs for boundary changes are based on only one fact: the Jews have not populated the Negev and established hundreds of settlements there. Had the Negev been settled with hundreds of thousands of Jews, even Nasser would never have dreamed of the possibility of rending it from the State of Israel. Wide and unpopulated expanses constantly and perpetually endanger the tranquility of the State. The Torah has already emphasized this notion when it states, "You shall not be allowed to quickly destroy them, so that the wild animals will not over-

whelm you" (Exodus 23:29). The fact that the Jews have
conquered the Negev is not enough, its settlement is
what is important. The great sage Maimonides ruled that
the first sanctification of the Land of Israel was not a lasting one because it was the result of a military conquest,
which was annulled by the violent attack of an enemy
whose army was vast and armaments numerous, who
conquered the Land and took it from us. The second
sanctification of the land, which was carried out through
occupation and settlement by Divine sanction, through
toil and sweat, was never annulled.[8] The sanctity that is
based on the settlement of the Land is, simply stated, for
now and for all time! We are terribly guilty for this gross
negligence. American Jewry could have certainly accel-
erated the process of colonization. Yet, why should we
examine the faults of others and place the responsibility
on the shoulders of nonobservant Jews? Let us admit our
own faults and confess to our own derelictions. Among
the Jews of America, Orthodox Jews bear the most
blame for the slow pace of the conquest of the Land
through settlement. It was for us, the loyalists of Judaism,
to heed the call of the Beloved more acutely, and to
respond to it immediately with extraordinary effort. In
commenting on the verse "And I shall lay desolate the
land" (Leviticus 26:32), Rashi[A] states in the name of
Midrash Torat Kohanim[B]: "This is a boon to Israel, that

[A] R. Solomon ben Isaac (1040–1105) classic commentator on the
Bible and Talmud.

[B] Compilation of rabbinic legal exegesis for the Book of Leviticus.

its enemies will not find tranquility in its land when it shall be bereft of its true inhabitants."The Land of Israel cannot be built by any other nation or people. Only the Jewish people have it within their power to settle the Land and make its desolation blossom. The Creator's promise was turned into a wondrous reality in different periods in the annals of the history of the Land of Israel. We cannot forget even for a moment, that the Land of Israel, like a magnet, attracted the nations of the world — both Christians and Muslims. The Crusades in the Middle Ages were undertaken with the purpose of conquering the Land of Israel and populating it with Christians. All the toil of the Crusaders was for naught. They did not strike roots in the Land. Even the indigenous Muslims did not succeed in properly settling the Land. It remained a barren desert, as is said, "And your land shall become a desolation" (Leviticus 26:33). Even in modern times, when European nations, in the seventeenth and eighteenth centuries, settled and populated entire continents, the Land of Israel remained desolate and in a more primitive state than its neighboring Arab lands: Egypt, Syria, and the Lebanon. Had the Land been settled by an industrious, successful, and cultured people, had the Land been properly populated and developed, our attachment to it would have been eroded by the course of events, and no Jewish foot would have trod upon it. Strangers would have eaten its bounty and its fruit, and our rights would have become null and void. However, the Land of Israel did not betray the Jewish people. It was loyal to them, awaiting redemption throughout the years. Logic dictates, then, that when the Jewish community was given the opportunity to return to its Land — which had withheld its treasures from foreigners and stored them for us — Orthodox Jews should have hastened to perform so great a mitzvah, to plunge with joy and enthusiasm into the very midst of this holy work: the building and settling of the Land. However, to our regret, we have not reacted that way. When the "desolate one," which longingly waited for us from era to era, invited us to come and redeem her from her desolation, and when the Beloved who watched over the desolation for almost nineteen hundred years, and decreed that during this time no tree should grow, and no wells should fructify the Land, beckoned at the door of the Lover, we the Orthodox Jews — the Lover — did not bestir ourselves from our beds to open the door for our Beloved. If we had contiguous settlements throughout the Land from Eilat to Dan, our situation would be very different.

Let us publicly and frankly confess: we complain about certain Israeli leaders and their attitude toward the values of our tradition and religious practice. The complaints are justified. We have serious charges against the secular leadership of the Land of Israel. However, are only they to be blamed, and are we as faultless and pure as the heavenly angels? Such an assumption is without foundation. We could have extended our influence and done something to shape the spiritual character of the Land if we had but hurried to awaken from our slumber and open the door for the Beloved who is knocking. I fear that we Orthodox Jews are still enveloped in sweet slumber. If we were to establish more religious kibbutz-im, if we were to build more housing for religious immi-grants, if we were to establish an extensive system of schools, our situation would be completely different. Then there would be no need to come forward with complaints against the leaders of other movements. We Orthodox Jews suffer from a unique illness that is not found in nonreligious Jews (with some rare exceptions). We are all miserly. We do not excel when it comes to giv-ing generously, in comparison with the rest of American Jewry. We are satisfied to part with a couple of pennies, and we demand, in recompense for our piddling dona-tion, our reward in this world and a share in the first allo-cations. Thus, our dignity has reached its nadir, and we do not exercise appropriate influence on Jewish life here in America and on the course of events in Israel. Great and free America is a land of charity. The govern-ment itself, in the years 1945 to 1956, disbursed $55 bil-lion, $350 million in foreign aid projects (the numbers are truly beyond our comprehension), and philan-thropists are truly respected in this land that knows how to give and help in such proportions. Accordingly, we Orthodox Jews are not entitled to the greatness that oth-ers possess. Lately, we have become experts at criticism and fault-finding. ("And the priest shall look on him, and pronounce him unclean" [Leviticus 13:3]). We know well how to criticize, to look for blemishes and to express opinions as self-styled experts. One thing, however, escapes us, and that is that the priest who pronounces defilement must leave the encampment to be with the afflicted sufferer so as to purify him. "And the priest shall leave the encampment ... and the priest shall command" (Leviticus 14:3–4). We must build not just a few small nooks, whose impact is unfelt, but central institutions throughout the length and breadth of America and the Land of Israel. We have an obligation to purify those who are "outside the encampment," who are situated in the huge camp of ignorance. To this end, there is a need for vast sums; and we, the Orthodox Jews, are far from being generous and charitable. For this reason, our institutions here and in Israel suffer from want. The Religious Zionist movement especially has to content itself with paltry sums. Due to lack of funds, the movement cannot function appropriately. Indeed, the loyal Lover is quite splendid, her eyes are like twin doves and her face radiates a beautiful charm (Song of Songs 1:15, 4:1). She is much fairer than the nonreligious lover. However, beauty is vain and grace is deceptive (Proverbs 31:30) if this Lover is stingy and very lazy. "I have removed my cloak, how shall I put it on again?" (Song of Songs 5:3). When one calls a rich Jew and asks him to give to a just cause, he answers, "I am going to Florida, and this year I have decided to stay in a luxury hotel, and I don't have the wherewithal to give you what you requested." What did the scholar tell the King of the Khazars? "You have embarrassed me, King of Khazars! . . . And our saying 'worship at His holy hill' [Psalms 99:9] is but the chirping of a starling" (*HaKuzari* 2:24). Do we not hear in our trembling over the safety and tranquility of the Land of Israel in our day, the beckoning of the Beloved who begs the Lover to let Him in? He has already been beckoning for eight years, and still He has not been properly responded to. Nonetheless, He continues to beckon. To our good fortune, our inherited Land has become more beautiful. The Beloved has not shown the Lover any favoritism, but He has compassion for her. The Beloved beckoned for only a short moment that night and disappeared, yet with us He has exhibited extraordinary patience. It is eight years that He has continued to beckon. Hopefully, we will not miss the opportunity!!

Chapter 6
The Covenants of Sinai and Egypt

When we delve into our historical existence we come to an important realization regarding our *Weltanschauung*. The Torah relates that the Holy One concluded two Covenants with Israel. One Covenant was made in Egypt. "And I shall take you unto Me for a people, and I will be to you a God" (Exodus 6:7). The second Covenant was at Mount Sinai. "And he [Moses] took the book of the covenant . . . and he said: 'Behold the blood of the covenant which the Lord made with you in agreement with all these words' " (Exodus 24:7-8). (The third Covenant, in the Book of Deuteronomy (28:69), is identical in content and purpose to the Covenant of Sinai.)[9] What is the essence of these two Covenants? It appears to me that this question was already answered at the beginning of our essay. Just as Judaism distinguished fate from destiny in the realm of personal individuality, so it also differentiated between these two concepts in the sphere of our national-historical existence. The individual is tethered to his nation with bonds of fate and chains of destiny. In accordance with this postulate, one can say that the Covenant of Egypt was a Covenant of Fate, and the Covenant of Sinai was one of destiny.

What is the Covenant of Fate? Fate signifies in the life of the nation, as it does in the life of the individual, an existence of compulsion. A strange force merges all individuals into one unit. The individual is subject and subjugated against his will to the national fate/existence, and it is impossible for him to avoid it and be absorbed into a different reality. The environment expels the Jew who flees from the presence of God, so that he is awakened from his slumber, like Jonah the prophet, who awoke to the voice of the ship's captain demanding to know his personal national- religious identity.

The historical loneliness of the Jew percolates from a feeling of compulsive fate. He is as alone in his life on earth as in his death. The concept of *kever yisrael*[A] emphasizes the Jew's strange detachment from the world. Sociologists and psychologists may say what they wish about the inexplicable isolation of the Jew. Their explanations are nothing more than barren speculation, incapable of rationally describing the phenomenon. Jewish separateness belongs to the framework of the Covenant of Fate that was concluded in Egypt. In truth, Judaism and withdrawal from the world are synonymous. Even before the exile in Egypt, separateness descended upon our world with the appearance of the

---

[A] Lit. Jewish grave. The author is referring to the religious requirement of burial in a cemetery consecrated solely for the use of Jews.

first Jew, our father Abraham. Abraham the Hebrew
(*ivri*) lived apart. "The whole world was on one side
(*ever*), and he on the other side" (Bereshit Rabbah 42:8).
Balaam, when he gazed upon the Israelite camp, understood the wonder of the experience of Jewish separateness and proclaimed with amazement: "They are a
nation dwelling alone and shall not be reckoned among
the nations" (Numbers 23:9). Even if a Jew reaches the
pinnacle of social and political accomplishment, he will
not be able to free himself from the chains of isolation.
Paradoxical fate watches over the isolation and uniqueness of the Jew, despite his apparent integration into his
non-Jewish environment. Even people of power and
authority, such as Joseph, the regent of Egypt, was separated from Egyptian society and remained alone in his
tent. "And they served him [Joseph] by himself . . . and
for the Egyptians . . . by themselves." (Genesis 43:32).
(Egyptians could not eat with the Hebrews, because it
was a taboo for them). Before his death Joseph pleaded
with his brothers, "When God will surely remember you
and bring you out of this land, you shall carry up my
bones from here" (Genesis 50:25). For despite my greatness and glory I am tied to you and your existence both
in life and in death. This singular, inexplicable phenomenon of the individual clinging to the community and
feeling alienated from the outside world was forged and
formed in Egypt. There Israel was elevated to the status
of a nation in the sense of a unity[10] from which arises

uniqueness as well. The awareness of the Fate Covenant in all of its manifestations is an integral part of our historical-metaphysical essence.

When the exclusive fate-driven individual stands face to face with God, he encounters the God of the Jews, who is revealed to man by the experience of loneliness and from the inexorability of existence — from the fate awareness that overcomes and subjugates man. He is the Almighty who does not wait for the supplications of man and his voluntary summons. He imposes His sovereignty upon him against his will. A Jew cannot banish the God of the Jews from his world. Even if he desecrates his Shabbat, defiles his table and his bed, and tries to deny his identity, he will not escape the dominion of the God of the Jews, which follows him like a shadow. So long as a person's physiognomy testifies to his birth, so long as Jewish blood flows in his veins, and so long as his flesh is Jewish, he is compelled to serve the God of the Hebrews. There is no counsel or tactic that can oppose Him. Even if the Jew who spurns his people should soar to the farthest heavens, from there the hand of the God of the Hebrews shall reach him. Where shall the Jew go to flee the God of the Hebrews and where can he escape from His presence?

And they said: The God of the Hebrews has revealed Himself to us. Please allow us to take a three days' journey into the desert, and we shall deliver sacrifices unto God lest he smite us with pestilence or sword.

—Exodus 5:3

Failure to cleave to the commands of the God of the Hebrews results in punishment and the destruction of existence.

The Covenant of Fate is also expressed in positive categories that stem from the awareness of shared fate. There are four facets to this rare state of mind.

First, the awareness of shared fate appears as that of shared experience. We are all in the realm of a shared fate that binds together the different *strata* of the nation and does not discriminate between classes and individuals. Fate does not distinguish between nobility and commonfolk, between rich and poor, between a prince dressed in royal purple velvet and a poor man who goes begging from door to door, between a pious Jew and an assimilationist. Even though we may speak a mix of different languages, even if we are citizens of different lands, even if we look different (one being short and black, the other tall and blond), even if we live in different economic systems and under different living conditions (the one living in a royal palace, the other in a humble cave), we have but one fate. When the Jew in the cave is attacked, the security of the Jew standing in the courtyard of the king is jeopardized. "Do not think in your soul that you, from all the Jews, [will escape and]

shall flee to the palace of the king" (Esther 4:13). Queen
Esther robed in majesty and Mordechai wearing sack-
cloth were situated in the same historical nexus. "All
Israel are bound together (*haverim*)" (TB Sotah 37a). We
are all persecuted, or we are all saved together.

Second, the awareness of shared historical experience leads to the experience of shared suffering. A feeling of empathy is a basic fact in the consciousness of
shared Jewish fate. The suffering of one segment of the
nation is the lot of the entire community. The scattered
and separated people mourns and is consoled together.
Prayer, the cry, and the consolation were formulated, as I
emphasized above, in the plural. Supplications that
emerge from the depths of travail are not confined to
the suffering and affliction of the groaning individual.
They encompass the needs of the entire community.
When there is a sick person in one's house, one prays
not only for that person but for all the sick of Israel.
When one enters the house of a mourner to comfort
him and to wipe the tear from the bereaved's sad face,
he directs his words of condolence to "all the mourners
of Zion and Jerusalem."[B] The slightest disturbance in the
state of an individual or a sector of the people should
trouble all segments of the nation throughout their dis-
persion. It is forbidden and it is impossible for the individual to isolate himself from his fellow and not participate in his suffering. If the assumption of shared histori-

---

[B] The traditional Jewish mourner's greeting. *Cf.* TB Shabbat 12b.

cal experience is accurate, then shared suffering is its direct corollary.

One of the great preachers of the last generation put it well when he likened the people of Israel to the two-headed son about whom it was asked in the Talmud whether he would, as a dual-personality, take two shares of his familial inheritance or only one portion.[11] So too one may ask: Has the dispersal of the nation in the Diaspora, and its taking root in different surroundings, caused its spiritual disintegration, or has the unity of the people not been lost despite the fact it has grown many heads and speaks many languages, with different customs and diverse ways of life? In a word, is the Jewish Diaspora one or not? The answer, continued the preacher, to the question of the unity of the people is identical with the decision rendered in the *beit midrash*[C] to the litigant who asked about the status of the two-headed heir. Let them pour boiling water on the head of the one, said the Rabbi, and let us see the other's reaction. If the other screams in pain, then the two comprise one personality, and they shall receive one share of the inheritance. However, if the second does not feel the suffering of the first, then they are two individuals enfolded in one body, and they shall receive two shares of the estate.

With respect to the unity of the nation as well, one must firmly establish that so long as there is shared suffering, in the sense of "I am with him in his distress"

[C] Study hall.

(Psalms 91:15), there is unity. If the Jew, on whom Providence has shined Its countenance, and who believes that with respect to himself the sharpness of hatred has been removed, and estrangement from his surroundings has passed, nevertheless still feels the distress of the nation and the burden of its fate/existence, then his bond to the nation has not been severed. If boiling water is poured on the head of a Moroccan Jew, the prim and proper Jew in Paris or London must scream, and by feeling the pain, shows himself loyal to the nation. The breakup of the people and the constriction of its self-image are the result of a lack of empathy.

Third, shared suffering is expressed in a feeling of shared obligation and responsibility. When the children of Israel left Egypt, Moses and Aaron fell on their faces, pleaded before God, and said: "Lord, God of Hosts of all flesh, shall one man sin and You direct divine wrath at the entire congregation?" (Numbers 16:22). This prayer accomplished that which the "shepherds of Israel" (Ezekiel 34:2) sought. The Holy One agreed with their action and only punished Korah and his cohorts. However, God only demonstrated this loving-kindness momentarily. Forever after, the "I" is ensnared in the sin of his fellow, if he had it within his power to reprimand, admonish, and bring his neighbor to repentance. The people of Israel have a collective responsibility, both halakhic and moral, for one another. The discrete units coalesce into a single halakhic-moral unity, with one all-encompassing and normative conscience and consciousness. The halakhah has already decreed that "all Jews are sureties for one another" (TB Shavu'ot 39a), such that one who has already fulfilled his personal mitzvah is not considered fully absolved thereby and may therefore fulfill the obligation on behalf of others who have not as yet done so. The "I" is not exempt from its obligation so long as his neighbor has not fulfilled that which is incumbent upon him. There is a special covenant of mutual responsibility among the children of Israel. This covenant is expressed in the blessings and imprecations pronounced on Mounts Gerizim and Ebal (Deuteronomy 11:29). It is based upon the notion of peoplehood revealed to Moses in Egypt. Out of this concept grew the covenant of mutual obligation. Moses, the dean of all prophets, in relating this covenant of mutual obligation, emphasized: "For that He may establish you today unto Him as a people, and He shall be unto you as a God" (Deuteronomy 29:12). He thus returned to the formulation of the Covenant of Egypt. "And I will take you to Me as a people, and I will be your God" (Exodus 6:7). Here the notion of shared fate was elevated from the plane of communal-political suffering to that of halakhic and moral responsibility. We are all sureties for one another, as it is said: "And the revelations belong to us and to our children forever" (Deuteronomy 29:28).[12]

Sharing of responsibility is not simply a halakhic-speculative notion, but a central fact in the history of Israel's relations with other nations. Our neighbors perpetually blame us for the transgressions of our co-religionists, and they turn the Talmud's rhetorical question of, "[If] Tobias sins; should Zigud be whipped?" (TB Pesahim 113b), into an everyday reality that no one questions. The identification of the activities of the individual with the deeds of the nation is a fundamental truth of the history of our people. Our enemies do not allow the individual Jew to remain alone in his own confines. They take him out of his own four cubits into the public domain and there harshly criticize the [entire] community because of him. This "standard" is only employed in relation to Israel and not with respect to other nations. No one has yet accused a Russian or a Chinese individual of being an agent of international communism and then held him liable, by virtue of his national origin, for the nations that lead the communist regime and aspire to subjugate the world under this cruel order. In contrast to this logical and humane approach to the members of other nations, the Jewish people as a whole is slandered, because of a handful of Jewish apostates, [with the allegation] that it is sympathetic to communism. We have yet to be absolved from this libel. Once again, the explanations of the experts for this phenomenon are not satisfactory. It makes no difference whether the causes are found in the realm of psychopathology or in the sphere of social history. Scientific classification is beside the point; the phenomenon remains obscure and inaccessible. We Orthodox Jews have one solution to this riddle: the hand of the Covenant of Fate, which was concluded in Egypt on the basis of the absolute uniqueness of the nation, is revealed amidst such an unintelligible reality.

The commandment to sanctify God's Name and the prohibition against desecrating it[13] are clear in light of the principle of shared responsibility and obligation. The activity of the individual is debited to the account of the many. Every wrong committed by an individual stains the name of Israel throughout the world. The individual is responsible not only for his own conscience but also for the collective conscience of the nation. If he conducts himself properly, he has sanctified the name of the nation and the name of the God of Israel; if he has sinned, he causes shame to befall the nation and desecrates its God.

Fourth, shared experience is expressed by cooperation. The obligation to perform acts of charity (*tzedakah*) and loving-kindness (*hesed*) is derived from the experience of unity that is so all-pervading and encompassing. When the Torah deals with these precepts it uses the term "brother" rather than "friend."

> And if your *brother* shall become impoverished . . . you shall support him . . . and he shall live among you.
> —Leviticus 25:35 (emphasis added).

Do not harden your heart, and do not shut your hand against your needy *brother* . . . open your

hand to your poor and destitute *brother* in your
land.
                    —Deuteronomy 15:7, 11 (emphasis added)

Confrontation with the fateful reality of the nation in all
of its strangeness instills the Jew with his common
awareness in the realm of social activism. The shared situation of all Jews, whether in the objective realm, as an
event, or in the subjective realm, as suffering, taps the
sources in the individual's soul for loving-kindness and
pity for his brethren, who are in trouble and that in a
roundabout way touches him as well. Maimonides formulated this idea in his laconic but content-filled manner.

> All Jews and those attached to them are like
> brothers, as it is said, "You are sons to the Lord
> your God" (Deut. 14:1), and if a brother will not
> show mercy to his brother, then who will have
> mercy on him? And to whom can the poor of
> Israel look for help — to those other nations who
> hate and persecute? They can look for help only
> to their brethren.[14, D]

From [both] the midst of a heritage which is compulsive and fateful and a terrible aloneness which are
the source of the unity of the nation, issues forth the

[D] *A Maimonides Reader*, ed. I. Twersky (New York, 1972), p. 135.

attribute of loving-kindness which summons and drives the fateful collective to imbue their unity with positive content by means of the constant participation in events, suffering, consciousness and acts of mutual assistance. The isolated Jew finds his solace in his active adhesion to the whole and by tearing down barriers of egotistical-separatist existence, and by joining his neighbors. The oppressive experience of fate finds its connection in the coalescing of individual personal experiences into the new entity called a nation. The obligation of love for another person emanates from the self-awareness of the people of fate, which is alone and perplexed by its uniqueness. For this was the Covenant of Egypt concluded.

Chapter 7
The Covenant of Destiny

What is the Covenant of Destiny? In the life of a people (as in the life of an individual), destiny signifies an existence that it has chosen of its own free will and in which it finds the full realization of its historical existence. Instead of a passive, inexorable existence into which a nation is thrust, an Existence of Destiny manifests itself as an active experience full of purposeful, movement, ascension, aspirations, and fulfillment. The nation is enmeshed in its destiny because of its longing for an enhanced state of being, an existence replete with substance and direction. Destiny is the font out of which flow the unique self-elevation of the nation and the unending stream of Divine inspiration that will not run dry so long as the path of the People is demarcated by the laws of God. The life of destiny is a directed life, the result of conscious direction and free will.

While the Covenant of Egypt was concluded without the consent of the people of Israel (the Holy One took them unto Him before He consulted with them: "And I will take you unto Me as a people" (Exodus 6:7)), the Covenant of Sinai was offered to them before it was promulgated. The Holy One sent Moses to tell them His message, and Moses returned to the Holy One with the people's answer. The halakhah perceives the Covenant of Sinai as a contract which is valid if written with the consent of the obligated party, in this case, the community of Israel. The proclamation that "We shall do and we shall hear" (Exodus 24:7) is the foundation of the Torah.[15]

What is the content of the Covenant of Sinai? It is a special way of life that directs the individual to the fulfillment of an end beyond the reach of the man of fate — the striving of man to resemble his Creator via self-transcendence. The creative activity that fulfills the Covenant of Destiny flows from a totally different source, from man's rebellion against an "as is," factual existence, and from the longing that impels him to more enhanced and sublime forms of existence. Acts of loving-kindness and fraternity, which are integrated into the framework of the Covenant of Sinai, are motivated not by the strange sense of loneliness of the Jew, but by the sense of unity experienced by a nation forever betrothed to the one God. The absolute oneness of God is mirrored in the unity of the nation that is eternally bound to Him. "You are One, and Your name is One, and who is like Your people Israel, One nation".[A] The essence of Jewish fellowship on this level is a byproduct of the father-son relationship between the members of the nation and God. (Maimonides already emphasized

---

A *Amidah*, Shabbat Afternoon Service, *cf.* Zechariah 14:9 and II Samuel 7:23.

this motif in the passage we quoted above.) At Sinai, God elevated the Covenant of Fate, which He had concluded with a collective that was forced to be alone and that practiced loving-kindness to others as a result of its requisite isolation, to a Covenant of Destiny with a collective of people of free will and volition that directs and sanctifies itself to confront the Almighty. He transformed the "people" — an amalgam bereft of direction and purpose — to a "nation," a term that signifies a distinct communal profile, a national physiognomy,[16] as it were. The people of loving-kindness was elevated into a holy nation.[17] The basis of shared destiny is the sanctity that is formed from a distinctive existence.[18]

When the man of destiny stands before the Almighty, he envisions the God of Israel who reveals Himself only with man's approval and invitation. The God of Israel is united with the finite creature only after man has sanctified and cleansed himself from all pollution, and longingly and agitatedly awaits this wondrous encounter. The revelation of the God of Israel does not come, in any event, in all conditions and circumstances. It demands a special state of spirit and soul, in the manner of "Be ready for the third day" (Exodus 19:11). Without the readiness of man, the God of Israel will not reveal Himself. He does not surprise His creatures. He responds to man's urgent petition. However, when man does not actively long for God with spiritual intensity, then the God of Israel shows no interest in him. When the God of the Hebrews chases after man against his will, He does not ask him for his opinion or desires. The God of Israel, however, consults with a person before an encounter. Already in Egypt the Holy One revealed Himself to Moses not only as the God of the Hebrews but also as the God of Israel who waits for man and invites him to His service to do His work. "So said the Lord, the God of Israel: Let my people go, that they shall make a feast unto Me in the wilderness" (Exodus 5:1).

Chapter 8
Encampment and Congregation

In order to explain the difference between a People of Fate and a Nation of Destiny it is appropriate to deal with a different contrast — that between an Encampment and a Congregation. The Torah used both of these concepts with respect to Israel. "Make for yourself two silver trumpets of hammered work; and they shall be to summon the *congregation* and for causing the *encampments* to set forth" (Numbers 10:2, emphasis added).

Encampment and Congregation constitute two different sociological experiences, two separate groups that have nothing in common and do not support one another. An Encampment is created out of a desire for self-defense and thrives on fear. A Congregation is fashioned out of longing for the realization of an exalted moral idea and thrives on love. In the Encampment, fate's rule is unlimited, whereas destiny rules the Congregation. The Encampment represents a phase in the development of the nation's history. The continued survival of a people is identified with the existence of the Congregation.

An Encampment, in its essence, is not a uniquely human phenomenon; one finds its traces in the animal kingdom as well. There, too, the encampment serves as a shield against outside danger. When fear of attack grips herds of cattle and sheep, they tumble down in a crazed frenzy from every green mountain and grassy place and run toward each other, lock horns, and butt their heads. Fear finds its instinctive expression in a common quest for protection through gathering together. The secret of individuals uniting into one camp in the face of peril is well known to the animal instinct.

In man's world too, an Encampment is created solely from fear. When fateful, choiceless existence terrifies man, the individual grasps the inadequacy of his strength and aligns himself with others for purposes of self-defense, in order to prevail over a common enemy. The establishment of an Encampment is a stratagem of warfare. Learn what the Torah has taught: "When you shall go out as an *encampment* against your enemy" (Deuteronomy 23:10, emphasis added). An Encampment is born out of the terror of destruction and loss, from the fear that fate is overwhelming. From the midst of the Encampment, the People arises. In the beginning, the Jews in Egypt were an Encampment. When they were freed by the Holy One, they rose to the level of a nation.

Indeed, the Congregation has a special place in the kingdom of man and in his mighty spirit. The Congregation is man's characteristic creation, and his glorious *persona* hovers over it. The Congregation is not created as a result of negative causes or out of fear of the fate that pursues man, who senses his own misery and feebleness, but rather as a result of positive impulses. Destiny is the foundation of the Congregation. A Congregation is a collection of individuals with a single past, a common future, shared aspirations, identical yearnings for a world that is totally good and pleasant, and a singular and harmonious destiny. The beginnings of the Congregation are embedded in the tradition of the people's ancestors at the dawn of its existence. Its end is rooted in a common vision of the end of days. The people of the Congregation are *witnesses*[19] to the events that have passed and to the miraculous future that has not yet arrived.[A] The Congregation encompasses not only those who are alive today but everyone who has lived and who will live from the dawn of humanity until the end of days. The dead who have passed on are still alive within the confines of the Congregation, and those destined to be born are already alive within its jurisdiction. A Congregation is a holy nation that does not fear fate and does not live against its will. It believes in its destiny and of its free will sanctifies itself for its realization. The Covenant of Egypt was made with a people that was born in the Encampment, the Covenant of Sinai was concluded with a holy people.

[A] The Hebrew words *edah* (congregation) and *ed* (witness) share the same root letters. They are here used as related etymologically.

Chapter 9
Conversion by Circumcision and Immersion

The integration into the fate and into the destiny of the chosen nation/people cannot be separated from the experience of belonging to *knesset yisrael*[A] as an integrated whole whose historical existence embodies the dual ideas of loving-kindness and holiness. The Covenant of Sinai completed the Covenant of Egypt. Destiny joined fate; together they became a distinct covenantal unit. It is impossible to separate these constituent parts and formulate an outlook that opposes the unity of a nation of loving-kindness to that of a sanctified people. A Jew who participates in the suffering of his nation and its fate, but does not join in its destiny, which is expressed in a life of Torah and mitzvot, destroys the essence of Judaism and injures his own uniqueness. By the same token, a Jew who is observant but does not feel the hurt of the nation, and who attempts to distance himself from Jewish fate, desecrates his Jewishness.[20]

A gentile who wishes to join the nation must take upon himself both covenants. He places himself in the

---

[A] The Congregation of Israel, i.e. the Jewish People as a totality.

ambit of Jewish fate and sanctifies himself for the acceptance of the Jewish destiny. The act of conversion
involves associating oneself as a member of the people
of the Covenants of Egypt and of Sinai. Keep this important principle in mind: there is no such thing as partial
conversion. One cannot omit one *iota* of either of these
two Covenants. Total devotion to the Jewish people — as
a nation that God took to Himself in Egypt, with all its
tribulations, suffering, responsibilities, and actions; and
as a holy people that is itself consecrated, heart and soul,
to the God of Israel and His halakhic and moral demands
— is the absolute foundation of Judaism and hence is
also the basis of conversion.

For this reason, halakhah dictates that a convert who
has been circumcised but has not yet immersed himself
in a *mikveh*,[B] or who has immersed himself and has not
yet been circumcised, is not fully converted until he
does both. Circumcision, which was given to Abraham
the Hebrew, the father of Jewish fate, and which was fulfilled in Egypt prior to the offering of the Paschal sacrifice — the symbol of the redemption from Egypt — signifies the fateful otherness of the nation, its necessary
isolation and uniqueness. Circumcision is a sign sculpted
into the very physical being of the Jew. It is a constant,
indelible sign between the God of the Jews and His people, one that cannot be erased. If the Covenant of Fate is
not sealed in the flesh, then the singularity of people-

[B] A ritual bath.

hood is absent and the gentile remains outside the bounds of the Covenant of Egypt.

Immersion in a mikveh, in contrast to circumcision, represents the integration of man into his great destiny and his entry into the Covenant of Sinai. The Jews were commanded to immerse themselves prior to the giving of the Torah at Sinai.[21] Immersion purifies and elevates from the profane to the holy, from life as it is to a life filled with a sublime vision. When the convert emerges from the waters of the mikveh, a new spiritual reality replete with destiny fills him, and he is endowed with the sanctity of the Jew (*kedushat yisrael*). It is not coincidental that the act of accepting the yoke of the commandments is tied to immersion.[22] The entire essence of immersion is the re-creation of the experience of the acceptance of the Torah and the elevation of the people to the status of a holy nation through its freely given commitment to obey God's word. If the convert is circumcised and does not immerse himself, then the association of man to destiny is missing, and the gentile is fenced off from the Covenant of Sinai and from a halakhic identification with a holy nation.

The formula for conversion in the Book of Ruth contains these two aspects, and their essence lies in the four final words of Ruth to Naomi: "Your people shall be my *people*, and your *God* my God" (Ruth 1:16, emphasis added).

Chapter 10
Mournful Thoughts of Confession

Let us pose a simple question: Did we not sin with respect to the first covenant, the Covenant of Shared Fate (as in the Covenant of Encampment-Nation), with regard to our obligation to participate in the pain of the nation and to see and feel its suffering: as it is said, "And He witnessed their burdens" (Exodus 2:11)? Let us be honest. During the terrible Holocaust, when European Jewry was systematically destroyed in gas chambers and crematoria, the American Jewish community did not rise to the occasion, and did not acquit itself as a community with the collective consciousness of shared fate, shared suffering and shared action with which it should have been expected to act. We did not properly sense the suffering of the nation, and we did precious little to save our unfortunate brethren. It is hard to know what we could have accomplished had we been more active. I personally think we could have saved many. No doubt, however, if we had properly felt the pain of our brothers; had we raised our voices and shaken worlds, that Roosevelt issue a sharp warning of protest accompanied by action, we would have been able to significantly slow the process of mass destruction. We witnessed the most

horrible tragedy in our history, and we were silent. I shall
not now dwell on the particulars. It is an extremely
painful chapter. We all sinned by our silence in the face
of the murder of millions. Do we not all stand before
God's seat of judgment charged with the grievous sin of
"You shall not stand idly by the blood of your neighbor"
(Leviticus 19:16), especially when the sin applies not
only to one individual but to millions? When I say "we" I
mean all of us: including myself, the members of rabbinic
and lay organizations both Orthodox and secular, and
Jewish political organizations of all persuasions. "Your
leaders, tribal heads, elders, and policemen, every person
in Israel . . . from the hewers of your wood to the draw-
ers of your water" (Deuteronomy 29:9–10). Do you
know why we were so indifferent? I think it is because
our sense of nationhood was damaged. We did not grasp
the notion of the experience of Shared Fate and the
essence of peoplehood. We were missing the attribute of
loving-kindness that Job, at first, also lacked. Job, who
suffered, was devoid of a sense of shared experience and
therefore did not know how to pray for his brothers. His
concern was only for his own and his family's well-
being. We were also devoid of the sense of [the
Covenant of] Encampment-Nation and therefore did not
offer heart-felt prayers, nor did we take any bold mea-
sures to save our brothers.

In the crisis that the Land of Israel is [at present] passing through, Providence is again testing us. It is fitting
that we openly state that this matter does not just involve

Israel's political future. The evil intentions of the Arabs are not only directed against our national independence but against the continued existence of the Jewish presence in Israel. They aspire to exterminate (God forbid) the *Yishuv*[A] — men, women, children, infants, sheep, and cattle (cf: I Samuel 15:3). At a meeting of Mizrachi (the Religious Zionists of America), I repeated, in the name of my father (of blessed memory), that the notion of "the Lord will have war against Amalek from generation to generation" (Exodus 17:16) is not confined to a certain race, but includes a necessary attack against any nation or group infused with mad hatred that directs its enmity against the community of Israel. When a nation emblazons on its standard, "Come, let us cut them off from being a nation so that the name of Israel shall no longer be remembered" (Psalms 83:5), it becomes Amalek.[23] In the 1930's and 1940's the Nazis, with Hitler at their helm, filled this role. In this most recent period they were the Amalekites, the representatives of insane hate. Today, the throngs of Nasser and the Mufti have taken their place. If we are again silent, I do not know how we will be judged before God. Do not rely on the justice of the "liberal world." Those pious liberals were alive fifteen years ago and witnessed the destruction of millions of people with equanimity and did not lift a finger. They are liable to observe, God forbid, the repetition of the bloodbath and not lose a night's sleep.

[A] The Jewish community in the Land of Israel.

Come, let us pray "for our friends" (Job 42:10). Let us feel for the suffering of the *Yishuv*. We must understand that the fate of the Jews in the Land of Israel is our fate too. The Arabs have declared war not only on the State of Israel, but on the entire Jewish people. They are now the leaders and financial supporters of international anti-semitism. Let us overcome the foolish fears of dual-loyal-ty that our enemies have instilled in us. To begin with, it is always impossible to satisfy antisemites, and they will find fault in whatever we do. Second, the matter relates not only to the continued existence of a state, but to the physical salvation of masses of Jews. Is it not our sacred obligation to come to their aid? Is it forbidden for us to seek the security of the *Yishuv*? We are being put to the test of Job. We have been given the opportunity to pray, by virtue of deeds and self-sacrifice, for "our friends" (Job 42:10) — and our friend is the Jewish community in the Land of Israel. We must do but one thing: open the door to the beckoning Beloved, and immediately all dangers will disappear.

Chapter 11
The Vision of the Religious Zionist Movement: Loneliness and Separateness

What should be the relationship of religious Zionism to its secular counterpart? It seems to me that political, secular Zionism has failed by virtue of one basic error. It is based on a false assumption that was introduced into the Covenant of Egypt, the Covenant of Fate. Secular Zionism asserts that with the founding of the State of Israel, we became a people like all other peoples, and that the force of, "It is a people that shall dwell alone" (Numbers 23:9), was diminished. The extremists in this movement want to eradicate the idea of the shared fate (community and nation) of the Jews of the Diaspora with the Jews of the Land of Israel. This train of thought is not only philosophically and historically erroneous, it is mistaken practically. In [adhering to] the notion of equality with all peoples and unity with all, the representatives of the State of Israel have on many occasions showed themselves to be extremely naive. They have failed to properly evaluate specific circumstances and conditions and have not correctly understood the hid-

den motives of certain persons. Out of a childlike
naiveté, they put stock in people who later betrayed us,
and have been inordinately moved by smooth talk and
flattery. To my mind, in several instances Israel's foreign
policy has lacked a sense of self-respect, national pride,
prudence, and the strength to stand by its principles.

These mistakes are outgrowths of the primary error
made by secular Zionism when it wished to erase both
the feeling of isolation and also the phenomenon of
shared suffering from our history books. The beckoning
of the Beloved must open the eyes of all of us, even the
most confirmed secularists. The State of Israel was not
and will not be able to abrogate the covenant of, "And I
will take you unto Me as a people" (Exodus 6:7) and put
an end to shared fate, the source of Jewish aloneness.
The State of Israel is as isolated today as the community
of Israel has been during the thousands of years of its
existence. And perhaps the isolation of the State is more
pronounced than in the past because it is so clearly
revealed in the international arena.

> They plot with craft against Your people, And take
> counsel against Your treasured ones. They have
> said: "Come, and let us cut them off from being a
> nation; that the name of Israel may be no more in
> remembrance. For they have consulted together
> with one consent; against You do they make an
> alliance; the clans of Edom and the Ishmaelites;
> Moab, and the Hagrites; Gebal, Ammon, and

Amalek: Philistia with the inhabitants of Tyre; Assyria too joins forces with them; they give support to the Children of Lot. Selah.

—Psalms 83:4-9

Communist Russia together with the Vatican, Nehru, the student of Gandhi, together with the devoutly Catholic Franco,[A] the British Foreign Office with Chiang Kai-shek,[B] have all joined in the attempt to isolate Israel and are being assisted by [Israel's other] enemies in other lands. This conspiracy began specifically after the establishment of the State, at a time when many of Israel's leaders thought that the Jewish problem had been solved, that Jewish isolation had been eradicated and normality had been introduced into our existence. The assumption that the State of Israel has weakened antisemitism is erroneous. On the contrary, antisemitism has grown stronger and employs false charges against the State [of Israel] in the war against us all. Who can foresee the end of this antisemitic hatred? The Covenant of Egypt cannot be abrogated by human hands. We remain a scattered people, nonetheless attached one to another. Our fate is the fate

---

[A] Spanish military leader and fascist dictator: Chief of State 1939-47; regent of the Kingdom of Spain 1947-75 and Head of State until his death in 1975.

[B] Chinese army officer and leader of the Nationalist party (Kuomintang), head of the Nationalist Government 1928–1949 and President of the Republic of China (Taiwan) from 1950 to his death in 1975.

of the *Yishuv*, and conversely the fate of the *Yishuv* is our
fate. No segment of the Jewish Nation will delude itself by
"fleeing to the palace of the king more than all the Jews"
(Esther 4:13). Everyone must "pray for his friends" (Job
42:10). An American Jew must not be silent and rest until
the danger in which the State of Israel finds itself is
removed and passes. The inhabitants of the Holy Land
should not babble about the "New Jew" that has been fashioned there, one who has no connection with Diaspora
Jewry. We are all obligated to listen to the "Clarion Call of
the Beckoning Beloved" (Song of Songs 5:1).

Still, the error of the secular Zionists is graver than
just not understanding the true meaning of the
Covenant of Egypt, the Covenant of a Nation-Camp realized through shared fate and forced isolation. They also
sin against the Covenant of Sinai, the covenant of a
sacred community and people that finds expression in
the shared destiny of a sanctified life. Only religious
Zionism with its traditional and authentic perception
has the power to "repair the perverted" (Ecclesiastes
1:15). If you were to ask me how the role of the State of
Israel can best be described, I would answer that its mission is not to nullify the special loneliness of the community of Israel or to destroy the unity of its fate — in
this it will not succeed — but to raise the people of the
encampment to the level of a sacred community nation
and to turn Shared *Fate* into Shared *Destiny*. We must
remember, as we have already emphasized, that *fate* is
expressed, in essence, in the experience of life under

duress — in an inability to run away from Judaism, in being forced to suffer as a Jew. This, though, is not the ideal of the Torah or of our *Weltanschauung*. Our solidarity with the community of Israel, according to an authentic Jewish outlook, must not come from the conclusion of the Covenant of Fate—that of the Encampment-Nation possessed of a compelled existence to which we are subjugated by outside forces— but by the conclusion of a Covenant with a sacred community-nation of *Shared Destiny*. Man does not find the experience of fate satisfying. On the contrary, it causes him pain. The feeling of isolation is very destructive. It has the power to crush man's body and spirit, silence his spiritual powers, and stop up the wellsprings of his inner creativity. The feeling of isolation, in particular, troubles man because it is devoid of reason and direction. The isolated person wonders, for whom and for what? Isolation, which cleaves to man like a shadow, shakes his awareness and ability. An existence of destiny, which is based on the Covenant of Sinai, is different. This concept turns the notion of "nation" (a concept that denotes an ordained existential necessity, participation in blind pain, and a feeling of isolation devoid of meaning) into a "sacred people" and to the elevated station of a moral, religious community. Man draws from it strength and sustenance, creative power and a renewed joy in an existence that is free and rejuvenated.

Let us return to what we said above. How does destiny differ from fate? In two respects: fate means a compelled existence; destiny is existence by volition. Destiny is created by man himself, who chooses and makes his own way in life. Fate is expressed in a teleological sense, in a denuded existence, whereas destiny embodies purpose and objectives. Shared Fate means an inability to rebel against fate. It is, as with the tragedy of Jonah the prophet, about the lack of alternatives to escape the God of the Jews; "And God hurled a great wind into the sea, and there was a mighty tempest in the sea, so that the ship was about to break apart" (Jonah 1:4). Shared Destiny means having free will to strive for a goal (a decision freely willed to be sanctified to an ideal) and a yearning and longing for the Master of the Universe. Instead of the blind fate that pursued him, Jonah in the end chose the exalted destiny of the God of Israel. "I am a Jew, and I fear the Lord, the God of the heaven" (Jonah 1:9).

Albeit, even in the experience of Shared Destiny there is an element of separateness, but the apartness of destiny is totally different both in character and experience. It is not the negative sentiment that Balaam foresaw in his prophecy of "they are people which dwells alone" (Numbers 23:9), but rather the special awareness that Moses promised Israel in the last few hours before his death: "And Israel shall dwell in safety [separate and secure] by the fountain of Jacob" (Deuteronomy 33:28). In truth, this self-isolation is nothing but the aloneness of a glorious, strong, holy, and sacred existence. It is the isolation expressed in the singularity of a people, in its holy self-image and unique existential experience. It is loneliness that creates an individual spiritual personality. It is loneliness that demonstrates man's honor and his aloofness. It is the solitude of Moses, whose exalted spirit and sublime vision the people did not comprehend. It is the solitude of Elijah and the other prophets. It is the solitude of which Abraham spoke to his attendants when he said, "You sit here with the donkey, and the lad and I will go to *that* place, and we shall worship" (Genesis 22:5, emphasis added).[C] While man's isolation is a destructive feeling of inferiority that expresses self-negation, the solitude of man testifies to his greatness and sanctity — the greatness contained within himself and the sanctity that hovers in the recesses of his unique awareness. Isolation robs man of his inner peace; loneliness bestows upon man security, self-esteem, significance. and confidence — "separate and secure" (Deuteronomy 33:28).

Judaism has always believed, as we said at the outset, that man has it within his power to take fate into his

---

[C] The author is making reference to the following text from *Midrash Breshit Rabbah, Parsha* 56 s.v. (2) *Amar*, "[Abraham] asked Isaac: 'My son, do you see what I see [the sanctity of Mount Moriah]?' [Isaac] said to him, 'I do.' [Abraham then asked] his two lads, 'Do you see what I see?' They answered, 'No [we do not].' [Abraham then] said, 'Since the donkey does not see, and you do not see, you shall sit here with the donkey you people which is like a donkey. [i.e. We, who have an elevated vision and can comprehend the sanctity of God's holy Mountain, will go unto the Mountain, worship God, and then return to you here on this lower level of sanctity].' "Vilna edition (Jerusalem, Vagshal, 2000) p. 572.

own hands and shape it into the destiny of a free life, a life full of meaning and saturated with the joy of living, turning isolation into aloneness and disparagement into significance. For this reason Judaism places so great an emphasis on the principle of free will. [And] for this reason [Judaism] so appreciates the human intellect, which has it within its power to free man from his enslavement to nature and allow him to rule over his environment and its blind circumstances and subjugate it to his will. The Community of Israel is obligated to use this free will in all facets of life, and especially for the good of the State of Israel. If secular Zionism, in the end, comes to understand that the establishment of the State of Israel has not weakened the paradoxical fate of Jewish aloneness, but, on the contrary, that the incomprehensible state of, "I shall take you unto Me as a people" (Exodus 6:7) has become even more pronounced in the international arena, it must ask itself the age-old question: "What is your occupation; from where do you derive . . . and from what people do you come?" (Jonah 1:8). The question is asked in any event; if not by the Jew, then by the gentile. We must answer with pride that, "We fear the Lord, the God of the heavens" (Jonah 1:9). Our historic obligation today is to raise ourselves from a people to a holy nation, from the Covenant of Egypt to the Covenant of Sinai; from a compelled existence to an original way of life, permeated with morality and religious principles, that transcends history. We must go from being an Encampment to being a Nation. The task of religious

Zionism is to fuse the two covenants, the Covenant of Egypt and the Covenant of Sinai; the covenants of fate and destiny, of isolation and loneliness. This task entails self-perfection by suffering; the out-pouring of loving-kindness brought about by combining all the elements of the nation and uniting them in one community, "A nation unique in the land" (II Samuel 7:23), and the readiness to pray for one's friend and to feel his joy and his grief. The goal of this self-repair is the purposeful consecration of self and ascent to the "Mountain of God" (Psalms 15:1). One great goal unites us all. A single exalted vision captures our hearts. One Torah (Written and Oral) directs us all to a unified end — the fulfillment of the vision of aloneness and the vision of the sanctity of an Encampment/People that ascends to the level of a Community/Nation and ties its lot to the destiny that was proclaimed to the world in the words of our ancient father Abraham: "And I and the lad shall go unto that place and shall worship God and return to you" (Genesis 22:5).

The Author's (the "Rav's") Notes

1. See TB Berakhot 7a. R. Meir was of the opinion that Moses' request to understand suffering (why the good suffer and evildoers prosper) went unanswered. R. Johanan, in the name of R. Jose, disagrees with R. Meir. Maimonides, in the *Guide for the Perplexed*, follows the view that the Holy One enlightened Moses as to the workings of all existence. See *Guide for the Perplexed* 1:54: "This dictum — 'All My goodness' — alludes to the display to [Moses] of all existing things . . . that is, he has grasped the existence of all My world with a true and firmly established understanding." *Guide for the Perplexed*, trans. S. Pines (Chicago: University of Chicago Press, 1963), p. 124.

2. The *Rishonim* dealt with the removal of choice from man as a result of his being deeply enmeshed in sin. See Maimonides, *Hilkhot T'shuvah* 6:3, and Ramban *ad* Exodus 7:3, 9:12.

3. The connection between adversity and repentance was expressed in the mitzvah of sounding a warning with trumpets when adversity is about to befall the community. Maimonides (*Hilkhot Ta'anit* 1:1-4), states: "A positive Scriptural commandment prescribes prayer and the sounding of an alarm with trumpets whenever trou-

ble befalls the community. For when Scripture says,
'Against the adversity that oppresses you, then you shall
sound the alarm with trumpets' (Numbers 10:9), the
meaning is: Cry out in prayer and sound an alarm against
whatsoever is oppressing you, be it famine, pestilence,
locusts or the like. [And the Scribes teach us that we
must fast until we are pitied from heaven on every misfortune that shall befall us.]" Translation from I. Twersky,
A. Maimonides Reader (New York: Behrman House,
1972), pp. 113-114.

There are two unique mitzvot: (a) A positive mitzvah
of confession and repentance for every sin that man
commits. This mitzvah is explained in the biblical portion of Naso. "When a man or a woman shall [commit
any sin that men commit], they shall confess the sins
that they have done" (Numbers 5:6). Maimonides, in the
Sefer HaMaddah, dedicated ten chapters to this mitzvah, entitled Laws of Repentance. (b) There is a specific
mitzvah of repentance in an hour of misfortune, as
recorded in the above-noted passage concerning the
trumpets: "And when you go to war [in your land against
the adversary that oppresses you, then you shall sound
the alarm] ... and you shall be saved from your enemies"
(Numbers 10:9). In practice, the biblical obligation to be
aroused to repentance is accomplished by the sounding
of the trumpets, to which the Rabbis added the vehicle
of fasting.

Essentially, the obligation to repent is tied to the suffering of the community, as noted by the Mishnah: [that

repentance is called for] "For every misfortune that shall befall the community" (TB Ta'anit 19a and Maimonides, loc. cit.). Indeed, the obligation of the individual who finds himself in extremis to return to God is also derived from this Torah portion. The fact that the halakhah recognized the individual's fast as valuable, proves that the individual is obligated to repent in a time of trouble. According to Maimonides, there can be no fast devoid of repentance. In [*Hilkhot T'shuva* 1:9], Maimonides writes that "Just as the community fasts on the occasion of its adversity, so does the individual fast on the occurrence of his misfortune." Similarly, the *baraita* cited in TB Ta'anit 22b states: "The Rabbis taught: In the case of a city that was surrounded by hostile gentiles, or by an overflowing river, or a ship being tossed by a stormy sea, or an individual pursued by non-Jews or by thieves or by a hurricane, etc. [in all these instances one may sound a voice alarm on Shabbat]." Maimonides ruled accordingly in *Mishneh Torah*, *Hilkhot Ta'anit* 1:6 (it being understood that there is no sounding of the trumpet on a weekday for an individual who is being pursued). The trumpets are sounded only for communal adversity and not for individual misfortune. There are specific halakhot in tractate Ta'anit and in Maimonides' *Hilkhot Ta'anit*, chap. 5, that delineate the character of communal adversity. The *baraita* only sought to teach that an individual who finds himself in *extremis* may cry out (according to Maimonides even on the Shabbat). It is therefore established that the obligation of crying out is equally applicable to the individual and the community, and of what benefit is crying, if it does not issue forth from a soul that regrets its sins?

The difference between the general mitzvah of repentance and the obligation to repent in a time of adversity may be distilled in one detail: Repentance for sin is tied to the knowledge that one has sinned. So long as a man is not aware of his sin he has no obligation [to repent]. One cannot be obligated to obtain forgiveness without knowledge of the sin for which he repents. As the verse states, "If his sin, wherein he has sinned, be known to him [he shall bring for his offering a goat, a male without blemish](Leviticus 4:23, emphasis added). Knowledge of a sin obligates the bringing of a sin-offering. Similarly, with regard to repentance, man is not required to repent for those [misdeeds] that are hidden, but only those that are revealed to him. However, in a time of adversity, the sufferer must examine his deeds and inquire after his sins in order to repent for them. The essence of suffering confirms the existence of sin and commands man: find your sin and return to your Creator. Examining one's deeds is characteristic of the obligation of repentance which is tied to suffering.

We know that on fast-days courts would sit and examine the deeds of the inhabitants of the city. The Talmud (TB Megillah 30b) states: "From the morning a group . . . examines the deeds of individuals." Maimonides ([*Hilkhot Ta'anit*] 1:17) firmly establishes the halakhah:

"On each fast day undertaken by a community beset by troubles, the court and the elders should remain in session at the synagogue from the end of the morning service until midday, to examine into the conduct of the citizens and to remove obstacles to righteous living provided by transgressions. They should carefully search and inquire after those guilty of extortion and similar crimes." (Translation from I. Twersky, *Maimonides Reader*, p. 114). [Cf. TB Eruvin 13b, "And now that [man] is created let him examine his deeds, and we said he shall take hold of his sins."] The obligation to examine one's deeds relates to a time of misfortune. It appears that the special obligation to repent on Yom Kippur (as explained in Maimonides, *Hilkhot T'shuvah* 7:7 and in the *Sha'arei T'shuvah* of Rabbenu Yonah Gerondi) was established as a special obligation of repentance for undisclosed deeds and a requirement to examine one's deeds in order to reveal the dishonorable aspects of a man's life. In this regard the obligation of repentance on Yom Kippur coincides with the obligation of repentance in a time of suffering. Concerning these opportunities, the verse states: "Let us search and examine our ways and return to the Lord" (Lamentations 3:40).

4. These statements and what follows are based on the passage in TB Bava Batra [15a–b] that cites diverse views as to the generation and time in which Job lived.

5. TB Sanhedrin 94a.

6. Cf. Maimonides, *Hilkhot Melakhim* 1:9 and the gloss of Rabad thereon. However, Maimonides' approach

is directed to the period after the kingship was given to David [after having been taken from Saul] and not to King [Saul] who preceded him. Cf. I Samuel 13:13-14. The rending of the kingdom of Judah [for generations] thus began with Saul. He too could have made amends for his sin by repentance.

7. This notion is expressed by Rava, TB Sanhedrin 72a, "Amar Rava *mai ta'ama de-mahteret*, [etc.]"

8. Maimonides (*Hilkhot Bet HaBehirah* 6:16) states almost explicitly that the fact that the second sanctification has endured till today and will last forever is based on the same rationale that he used in relation to the question of the sanctity of the Temple that cannot be nullified. Physical destruction cannot exile God's Presence from among the ruins.

9. See *Yalkut Shimoni, Nitzavim*, s.v. *shalosh beritot*; TB Berakhot 48b and Rashi ad loc.

10. See the *Sefer HaShorashim* ["Book of Hebrew Roots"] of R. David Kimhi, *shoresh "im"* [lit. "with"]: "The import of this word is joining and cleaving ... and the word *am* derives from it ... since a collection of people and their joining together is called an *am*." [The two Hebrew words are spelled with the same consonants and differ only in the vowels appearing below the consonants.] Cf. Gesenius, *Hebrew and Chaldean Lexicon*, s.v. *am*.

11. Cf. *Tosafot*, TB Menahot 37a, s.v. *'o*. See also *Shittah Mekubbetzet* ad loc., par. 18.

12. TB Sotah 37b, TB Sanhedrin 43b, Rashi *ad* Deuteronomy 29:28.

13. See Maimonides, *Hilkhot Yesodai HaTorah* 5:11.

14. Maimonides, *Hilkhot Matnot Aniyyim* 10:2.

15. The Talmud states (TB Shabbat 88a): "One learns from this that the Holy One held the Mountain [i.e., Sinai] over their heads like an inverted cask." This expresses the notion that God proposed to the Jewish people that they accept the Torah and deliver themselves to Him out of their free will in order to live the life of a holy people, instead of a compelled existence of destiny, which is likened to being perpetually threatened by a mountain hanging over one's head like an overturned cask." Cf. Tosafot ad loc. s.v. *kafah* and *moda'ah*.

16. See R. Yonah Ibn Janah, *Sefer HaShorashim* (ed. A. Bacher), s.v. *goy*. See also R. David Kimhi, *Sefer HaShorashim*, "R. Jonah [Ibn Janah] said that the term *goy* [nation] is appropriate for [even] one person, as it says, 'Shall you slay even a righteous *goy*?'(Genesis 20:4)." See also (a) S. Mandelkern, *Concordance*. s.v. *goy*, where he states, "It refers to a group of people who belong to one nation that have formed a body [politic] (emphasis added)," and (b) Gesenius, *Hebrew Lexicon*, s.v. *goy*.

However, occasionally we encounter the term *goy* in relation to a group of animals, as in "For a *goy* [of locusts] has come up to my land" (Joel 1:6). It is understood that with regard to animals this term appears metaphorically. See (a) Radak and Rashi ad loc., and (b) R. Elijah of Vilna, *Commentary on the Bible, ad* Isaiah 1:4, "Ah, sinful nation, a people laden with iniquity," wherein he states:

"Now . . . the term *am* will be used with respect to the collective of a large number of persons, even a multitude, . . . but [the term] *goy* is used only for those who are law-abiding . . . as our Rabbis have said, ' "There he became a *goy*" (Deuterotomy 26:5). This teaches that the Israelites were distinctive there' [Passover Haggadah] [i.e., by their observance of traditional norms of behavior]."

17. The phrase *am kadosh* [holy nation] connotes a collective that has been elevated in holiness. It is essentially equal in essence to the term *goy kadosh* [holy people].

18. The uniqueness of the Jew began to be forged in the crucible of the affliction in Egypt. The historical suffering in Egypt fashioned the image of the nation as a people, possessing a special physiognomy and an individual nature that readied it for the sublime moment of the concluding of the Covenant of Destiny at Sinai. Scripture attests to the birth of the Jewish collective in Egypt. "An Aramean attempted to destroy my father [Jacob], then [Jacob] descended to Egypt . . . and there he became a nation" (Deuteronomy 26:5). How beautifully our Rabbis expounded this verse: "This teaches that the Israelites were distinctive there" [ibid.]. Nationhood and being "distinguished as a special collective" mean the same thing. Truthfully, the forging of a Nation-People was the purpose of the enslavement of our forefathers in Egypt. They descended as the sons of Jacob, and they left as a nation tied to God and a people destined to the rev-

elation of Providence and the conclusion of the Covenant of Destiny at Sinai. [As the *Zohar* says: "Similarly with [Jacob's descendants] whom God desired to make a unique and perfect people and to bring near to Himself: if they had not first gone down to Egypt and been tested there, they would not have been God's chosen people...." [*Zohar, Lekh Lekha* 83a (New York: Soncino Press, 1933, vol. 1, p. 276–277]. However, until they went out from Egypt they were not yet a nation and did not appear in a fitting light. As it is written: "As a rose among thorns so is my love among the daughters" (Song of Songs 2:2). The Holy One desired to shape Israel on the celestial pattern, so that there would be one rose on earth, [similar to the] rose in heaven. Now the rose, which gives out a sweet aroma and is conspicuous among all other roses, is the one that grows among thorns" [Ibid., *Ki Tissa* 189b, vol. 4, p. 138].

19. A congregation can also signify devotion to a negative ideology by people who sow evil. "And he shall not be as Korah and his congregation" (Numbers 17:5) [and] "All this evil congregation" (Numbers 14:35).

20. See Maimonides, *Hilkhot T'shuvah* 3:11, "One who secedes from the commonweal, even though he commits no transgressions other than separating himself from the congregation of Israel, and does not perform mitzvot in its midst and does not share in its suffering and does not fast on its fast-days, but goes his own way like a gentile who is not part of the congregation, has no portion in the world-to-come."

21. [I.] Maimonides [*Hilkhot Issurei Bi'ah* 13:1-3, based upon TB Keritot 9a] states explicitly that in Egypt there was no immersion required [for conversion], which took effect solely by means of circumcision. It was at Mount Sinai that the children of Israel were commanded to immerse themselves as part of the conversion process. As Maimonides says:

"With three [rituals] did the people of Israel enter the covenant: circumcision, immersion, and the offering of a sacrifice. Circumcision took place in Egypt, as it is written, 'But no uncircumcised person shall [eat of the Paschal offering]' (Exodus 12:48); [thus] Moses circumcised them. 'Immersion was in the desert before the giving of the Torah, as it is written, 'And sanctify them today and tomorrow, and let them wash their garments' (Exodus 19:10). "Maimonides interprets the talmudic statement (Yebamot 71a) that one may not convert through circumcision alone as referring solely to posterity, but not to the first Passover, where all agree that circumcision was sufficient to effect conversion. Similarly, Maimonides would explain the position of R. Joshua that immersion was required as part of the conversion of our forefathers as dating from the revelation at Sinai, in accordance with the plain import of the verses cited there (see Yebamot 46b, s.v. *R. Joshua*). However, Maimonides would concede that with respect to the women in Egypt immersion was required. As the Talmud states explicitly in that portion: "For it is impossible to defer the immersion of the women from the time of the liberation from Egypt to the revelation at Sinai." This is because of a powerful question that arose in the Talmud and was noted by Rashi (ad loc., s.v. *b'imahot*): "[This refers to] their wives who immersed themselves, as is explained below. For if they had not immersed themselves, by what act would they have entered under the wings of the Shekhinah?" In other words, they required some formal rite of conversion. Similarly, the Tosefta (TB Pesahim 8:18) asserts that the requirement that non-Jewish maid-servants immerse themselves prevented [their masters from] bringing the Paschal offering according both to the view stated in the Mishnah and that of R. Eliezer b. Ya'akov. Cf. Rabad, *Hilkhot Korban Pesah* 5:5.

In truth, we could maintain that immersion for males was also practiced in Egypt, and that at Mount Sinai the males were commanded to immerse themselves again because the giving of the Torah would endow them with an extra level of sanctity. Every act of conversion requires immersion, and the conversion in Egypt conformed to this general rule.

[Translator's note: A non-Jew who is acquired as a slave by a Jew must undergo immersion and circumcision. He thus acquires the status of a quasi-Jew and is obligated to perform some of the mitzvot. When the slave is freed and becomes a full-fledged Jew he requires a second immersion]. This view is supported by the position of many Rishonim, among them Maimonides, that the second immersion of a non-Jewish

slave [as part of his manumission] is a biblical requirement. This results from the slave's being endowed thereby with an added dimension of obligation to perform
mitzvot, through his elevation, as a free man, to the status of a full-fledged Jew. It is thus understandable, that
at Sinai, when the Jews embraced Torah and mitzvot,
they were required to undergo an additional immersion, aside from the one undergone in Egypt. Even
according to the view of *Nimmukei Yosef*, who holds
that the immersion of a manumitted slave is only rab-
binically ordained, the Jews at Sinai were nevertheless
required to undergo a second immersion. The case of a
slave, who was already [partially] converted through
circumcision and immersion and had thereby already
entered the Covenant, is different from that of the children of Israel at Sinai, who needed to be endowed with
an added dimension of sanctity which served as the
basis of the Second Covenant. Regarding the slave, in
the opinion of *Nimmukei Yosef*, there is no need [i.e.,
biblically] for an added act of immersion, because we
are dealing with the presence of an obstacle [to full
Jewish status, i.e., servitude]. Once the servitude is can-
celled through manumission, removing the obstacle
that precluded the slave from an obligation to time-
bound mitzvot as well as from marriage to a Jewish
woman, he lacks nothing [i.e., he needs no further formal act of conversion]. At Sinai, however, the Jews were
imbued with a new form of sanctity that had been
unknown before and thus were enjoined to perform a

second act of conversion. Therefore, they required a second immersion.

[II.] One could ask why the children of Israel were not required to undergo a second symbolic act of circumcision [*hatafat dam berit*; lit. "the letting of blood from the place of circumcision"] at Sinai. To this one could reply that circumcision (of a convert), which normally precedes immersion and (as noted above) does not generate a new dimension of sanctity, need not occur a second time on the occasion of an individual's acquiring added sanctity. We require simply that a proper act of circumcision be performed for a conversion to proceed. Thus, if the circumcision had already been performed, when the convert had entered into a lower degree of sanctity, we need not [symbolically] circumcise him again when he enters into a state of higher sanctity. So, too, the slave, when he is emancipated, he need not be circumcised even though he becomes obliged to perform new mitzvot and is raised up to a higher level of sanctity. This is because his first circumcision, undertaken for quasi-conversion [lit. "slavery conversion"] was properly performed. However, the immersion, which completes the conversion, and from which full Jewish status [*kedushat yisrael*, lit. "the sanctity of Israel"] issues, must be repeated when the convert ascends from a lower level of sanctity to one that is higher.

However, upon broader examination (of the Rishonim), how shall we account for the opinion of Nahmanides, who maintains (*novellae ad* Yebamot 47b, s.v. *nitrape*) that a convert who immerses himself, and only subsequently is circumcised, has undergone a perfectly valid conversion? In line with this opinion we would periodically encounter situations in which circumcision comes (after immersion) and thus at the end of the conversion process. If so, the elevating factor would be reversed, and we would be required to perform *hattafat dam berit* after the immersion since this would bring him to a higher degree of holiness and not the immersion.

However, note that Ramban [loc. cit.] asserts that even the members of the tribe of Levi, who had been circumcised prior to the Exodus from Egypt in fulfillment of the mitzvah [i.e., the one given to Abraham] and not for purposes of conversion, did not require *hattafat dam berit*, as he wrote:

"And if so, how did the tribe of Levi enter the covenant? They went through the process of *hattafat dam berit*. Yet it appears to me that as regards the requirement for circumcision, they did not require *hattafat dam berith* because they were already circumcised for the sake of the mitzvah of circumcision; unlike the circumcision of an Arab or a Gibeonite, who were not given the mitzvah of circumcision, and therefore are [legally] considered uncircumcised." It is apparent from Nahmanides' statement that circumcision is not as integral an act as immersion in the process of conversion. The object of circumcision is to remove the convert from the category of the uncircumcised. If he was not circumcised, he cannot become infused with *kedushat yisrael*, because an uncircumcised person may not enter the covenant. Accordingly, if the convert is circumcised, he need only immerse himself in order to convert. An Arab who was circumcised but not for the purpose of conversion is legally uncircumcised and must undergo *hattafat dam berit*. (See TB Nedarin 31b, Yebamot 71a, Abodah Zarah 27a.) However, the sons of Levi, who were descended from Abraham and were circumcised according to the command of the Holy One, were not enjoined to undergo *hattafat dam berit*.

In light of this suggestion [and employing the above supposition] we [are able to] resolve our question as to why recircumcision [*hattafat dam berit*] is not required when going to a higher state of sanctification according to the view of Nahmanides, who holds that at times conversion is completed with circumcision.

We have seen [as delineated above] that circumcision is not at all part of conversion. All circumcision does is remove the convert from the category of the uncircumcised. Therefore, one who is already circumcised [according to the halacha] does not require *hattafat dam berit* when he ascends from one level of sanctity to another level. Immersion is different because it instills *Kedushat Yisrael* and is thus an integral part of the conversion process. Therefore, when additional sanctity is to be added we require immersion but not *hattafat dam berit*. Nahmanides, however, is of the view that immersion can take place before circumcision, even though one does not become a full-fledged Jew immediately thereafter. It is, however, effective for the future. When the convert is circumcised [and the obstacle removed], his conversion and Jewishness take hold as a result of the prior immersion.

[III.] The basic question of whether circumcision is a part of the conversion process or merely removes the convert from the status of being uncircumcised is dependent upon a dispute among the Rishonim as to whether a *bet din* need be present at the time of the circumcision. From the manner in which Maimonides formulates his opinion, we can deduce that the presence of a *bet din* (religious court) is required only for the immersion. In line with this, one could argue that circumcision achieves nothing more than the removal of a legal bar to the conversion [See Hilkhot Issurei Bi'ah 13:6 and 14:5-6].

Tur and *Shulhan Arukh* note the necessity of the [formal] process of *bet din* for circumcision as well, and so it is explicitly stated in the *novellae* of Ramban (TB Yebamot 45b). If this is the case, our suggestion that Nahmanides views circumcision as simply the removal of the status of being uncircumcised is incorrect. The very fact that Nahmanides requires the presence of a *bet din* at the time of circumcision testifies that the act of circumcision is an integral act of conversion and therefore susceptible to the requirement for the presence of a *bet din*. The question thus rearises: Why did the tribe of Levi at Mount Sinai not undergo *hattafat dam berit*, since their original circumcision was not for the purpose of conversion?

(Nahmanides' view is actually similar to that of Tosafot [Yebamot 41b, s.v. *mi lo*], that immersion and circumcision are sufficient to fulfill the mitzvah of circumcision [and do not need to be done explicitly for the sake of conversion]. Nahmanides relied on the statement of the Jerusalem Talmud that he cited. This, however, will not provide a solution to our quandary. Circumcision and immersion for the sole purposes of fulfilling these mitzvot are acceptable for conversion only once the Torah was given and the halakhah of conversion was established requiring that conversion is accomplished through circumcision and immersion. In this framework, circumcision and immersion are effective even if performed solely in fulfillment of a commandment and not explicitly for purposes of conversion. However, the tribe of Levi, which was circumcised in Egypt before the people of Israel were given the mitzvah of circumcision for purposes of conversion, concluded an act of conversion through circumcision. This [pre-Sinaitic] act of circumcision can not effectuate the conversion which the Jews were later commanded to undergo at Sinai.)

It would appear that Nahmanides was of the opinion that circumcision constitutes an act of conversion only so long as it (is an halachally mandated circumcision) has not yet been fulfilled, but not after such a [legally binding act] has been performed. Circumcision as an act of conversion finds its expression only when the subject

lacks a legally valid circumcision. Therefore, a circumcised Arab who converts requires *hattafat dam berit*
because his previous circumcision is of no legal value.
Through *hattafat dam berit* he will fulfill the commandment to enter the covenant of our Father
Abraham, which is an integral part of the mitzvah of circumcision. However, the Levites who had fulfilled the
mitzvah of circumcision in all of its detail [which they
were mandated to perform] as descendants of Abraham
and flawlessly fulfilled their obligation, did not require
hattafat dam berit, for what more would they achieve
thereby?

It appears that Nahmanides was of the opinion that
circumcision constitutes an act of conversion so long as
the conversion process remains unfulfilled in its entirety. Circumcision is only a "converting action" when the
convert still lacks the full effectuation of his conversion.
For this reason, a circumcised Arab requires a ritual letting of blood because his original circumcision is of no
[legal] value, and with a ritual letting of blood the convert will achieve his entry into the covenant of our
Father Abraham, which is an integral part of the mitzvah
of circumcision. However, the Levites, who fulfilled the
mitzvah of circumcision *qua* descendants of Abraham, in
all of its details, and flawlessly fulfilled thereby their
obligation, did not require a ritual letting of blood, for
what more was to be achieved thereby? Therefore, their
conversion was, willy-nilly, limited solely to immersion,
as in the case of women and castrati. (Compare the man-

ner in which Nahmanides concludes his comment [loc cit.]: "Therefore, the children of Levi were judged to be in the same category as women, such that they were allowed to convert through immersion alone.") Therefore, when a [gentile slave belonging to a Jew] converts [and thereby is elevated] from a lesser to a greater level of sanctity, he does not require a *hattafat dam berit*, for was not the commandment of circumcision already fulfilled in its entirety. In contrast to circumcision, the role of immersion in the conversion process is not due to any commandment or requirement that needs to be satisfied. It has no legal significance aside from its role as effecting conversion. Immersion, as a means of imbuing *kedushat yisrael,* can take place any number of times, and wherever there is an increase in sanctity, one undergoes immersion.

22. The fact that the acceptance of the [obligation to perform] mitzvot (lit. *Kabbalat Ol Mitzvot*) is tied to the immersion which is an integral part of the conversion [process] is almost axiomatic, as is explained in Yebamot 47a-b and in Maimonides, *Hilkhot Issurei Bi'ah* 13:12 and 14:6–7. Rashi expresses this point explicitly. "For now, by the act of immersion, he effectively converts; hence at the time of the immersion he must accept the commitment to observe mitzvot" (lit. yoke of the commandments). However, Tosafot (Yebamot 45b, s.v. *me lo taula*) states that *kabbalat ol mitzvot* can occur before immersion.

Maimonides (*Hilkhot Issurei Bi'ah* 13:17) states: "A convert who was not questioned [as to whether he

would be faithful to the performance of the mitzvot] or
who was not informed of the mitzvot and the punish-
ments for transgressions, but who was circumcised
before a lower court of three is a convert." I once heard
from my father ([R. Moses Soloveitchik] of blessed memory) that Maimonides did not intend to say that a convert who converted with the intention of not fulfilling
the mitzvot is considered a true convert. Such a notion
would uproot the entire concepts of conversion and
kedushat yisrael, which [derive] from our obligation to
observe the mitzvot of God. Maimonides' opinion is that
the acceptance of mitzvot is not a distinct act in the conversion process that requires the oversight of a *bet din*
as does immersion, but is rather an overriding characteristic theme in the conversion process that is predi-
cated upon acceptance of the responsibility for observ-
ing mitzvot. Therefore, if we know that a convert by his
immersion is willing to accept the "Yoke of the Torah"
and mitzvot, even though there was no formal notifica-
tion of the mitzvot and formal acceptance by the convert, the immersion will be legally sufficient because the
convert intends to live the sacred life of a committed
Jew. [In contrast,] the Tosafot that we cited before seems
to maintain that the acceptance of the "Yoke of Mitzvot"
is a discrete act in the conversion process, and that the
requirement for the *bet din*'s involvement was restrict-
ed thereto. Immersion (according to this view) does not
require the presence of a *bet din*; only *kabbalat ol
mitzvot* must occur in its presence.

Nahmanides (Hiddushei HaRamban, Yebamot 45b) states: "Even a male convert who accepted the mitzvot prior to circumcision must do so again at the time of immersion." Ostensibly, it appears that in his opinion *kabbalat ol mitzvot* occurs at the time of [a prior] circumcision as well. However, one could interpret Nahmanides as not intending to refer to the acceptance of mitzvot as a discrete act, but as a general characterization of the act of circumcision. Circumcision must be fulfilled out of a commitment to mitzvot, as I noted above with respect to Maimonides' view. Maimonides, however, is of the opinion that the formal act of *kabbalat ol mitzvot* is not at all determinative. Maimonides agrees with the view of the Tosafists that there is a distinct act [of *kabbalat ol mitzvot*] and it requires the presence of a *bet din*. Aside from the special acceptance of mitzvot, the circumcision and the immersion must also be done out of a commitment to mitzvot, which is identical to conversion.

23. With respect to the seven nations of Canaan Maimonides wrote in *Hilkhot Melakhim* 5:4:

"It is a positive mitzvah to destroy the seven nations [of Canaan], as it is said: 'You shall utterly destroy them' (Deuteronomy 7:2), and anyone who encounters one of them and does not kill him has violated an injunction, as it is said, 'Do not keep alive a soul' (Deuteronomy 20:16), and [in fact] their memory has already been erased.

"Radbaz [R. David Ibn Abi Zimra, sixteenth century] located the source of the last line, "and their memory has already been erased," in the words of R. Joshua (M. Yada'im 4:4), "Sennacherib, king of Assyria, has already arisen and intermingled all of the nations" [i.e. so that none retained their distinct identity].

But note something strange: in relation to the destruction of Amalek, Maimonides does not add the words "and their memory has already been erased." In *Hilkhot Melakhim* 5:5, Maimonides writes:

"And similarly it is a positive mitzvah to erase the memory of Amalek, as it said: 'Erase the memory of Amalek' (Deuteronomy 25:19), and it is a positive mitzvah to forever remember his evil deeds and his laying ambush (against you), in order to arose anger against him. As it is said, 'Remember what Amalek did to you.' Tradition teaches: Remember — with your mouth; do not forget in your heart, for it is prohibited to forget his enmity and hatred."

From Maimonides' words it appears that Amalek still exists in the world, whereas the seven nations of Canaan have descended to the depths of oblivion.

One wonders why Maimonides did not employ the rule of R. Joshua that "Sennacherib came and intermingled all the nations" with relation to Amalek. The answer to this question is very simple. The Bible testifies that Amalek still exists in this world. Go and see what the Torah says: "The Lord will have war with Amalek from generation to generation" (Exodus 17:16). Accordingly, it is impossible for Amalek to be blotted out of the world until the coming of the Messiah. So said our Sages: "God's name and throne will not be complete until the children of Amalek are blotted out" (Rashi to Exodus 17:16). But where is Amalek? I heard the answer from my father of blessed memory. Every nation that conspires to destroy the Jewish people is considered by the halakhah to be Amalek. My father added that as concerns Amalek itself we were commanded to perform two mitzvot: (a) [for the individual] to blot out the memory of Amalek, which is incumbent on everyone [to slay] any individual member of Amalek [that he encounters], as expounded in the Torah portion of Ki Tetzeh, "You shall blot out the memory of Amalek" (Deuteronomy 25:19), and (b) [for the community] to engage in communal military preparedness for war against Amalek, as it is explained in the Torah portion of B'shalach, "The Lord will wage war with Amalek from generation to generation" (Exodus 17:16). With relation to any other nation that stands ready to destroy us, we are [now after the time of Sennacherib] commanded to wage war against it [even] while it prepares for war against us, and our war against it is a "War of Mitzvah", in accordance with the command of the Torah that "The Lord will wage war with Amalek from generation to generation." However, the destruction of individuals, which is derived from the Torah portion of Ki Tetzeh, refers only to the biological descendants of Amalek. The words of Maimonides include the obligation to wipe out individuals, which does not apply to any other nation that plots destruction against the People of Israel. However, since the obligation of warring with Amalek pertains to such a nation (as well), he did not employ the phrase "And its memory has already been lost." The status of Amalek exists even now after the nations were intermingled [by Sennacherib].

And perhaps this is the basis for Maimonides' view (*Hilkhot Melakhim* 5:1) that a defensive war by Jews against an enemy who comes to wage war against it is a "War of Mitzvah'. For this kind of war is subsumed by the notion "The Lord will have war against Amalek from generation to generation." To be sure, Maimonides especially singled out the war with Amalek [in that regard]; nevertheless, one may say that saving Jews from an enemy that has arisen to destroy them is encompassed to this Torah portion [i.e., the destruction of Amalek]. Cf., Sotah 44b, s.v. *amar R. Jochanan.*